W9-BWM-640

THE TASTE OF ASHES

THE TASTE OF ASHES

An Autobiography by

BILL STERN

With

Oscar Fraley

Illustrated with Photographs

HENRY HOLT AND COMPANY

NEW YORK

In Canada, George J. McLeod, Ltd.

Published, September, 1959
Second Printing, October, 1959
Third Printing, November, 1959
Fourth Printing, December, 1959
Fifth Printing, January, 1960

Library of Congress Catalog Card Number: 59-12903

88134-0119

Printed in the United States of America

To
my wife
HARRIET
whose unwavering love
and steadfast faith
transformed the end
into the beginning

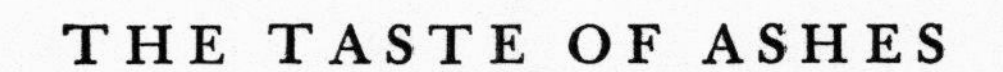

THE TASTE OF ASHES

Foreword

IT WAS A DAY OF SUNSHINE and laughter. The huge oval Sugar Bowl Stadium in New Orleans was packed with 83,000 fans this New Year's Day of 1956 to watch Georgia Tech play the football Panthers of the University of Pittsburgh.

Anticipation boiled over as the two teams spilled onto the field and the rival captains prepared to meet with officials. The opening kickoff was only minutes away.

These are always the moments of tension. Yet there was even more of an undercurrent than usual in the American Broadcasting Company radio and television booth perched high atop the concrete lip of the sprawling stadium.

Bill Stern, whose mellow, authoritative voice was to carry the game to countless millions from coast to coast, was late.

A moment later there was a sigh of relief as he burst into the booth, plunged to his seat, and took the signal from the engineer.

"Good afternoon, ladies and gentlemen. This is Bill Stern speaking from the Sugar Bowl in New Orleans where this afternoon we bring you the Sugar Bowl classic between Pittsburgh and Georgia Tech. The captains are going out on the field and here are the starting lineups:

For Pittsburgh, at left end, Joe Walton, two hundred and ten pounds, from Beaver Falls, Pennsylvania.

At left tackle, Bob Pollock, six feet, two inches, from Mount Carmel, Pennsylvania.

After these few opening words the tension in the booth rebuilt to a suffocating pitch.

Bill Stern, the man whose smooth, steady patter was radio legend, had begun to run down like an old-fashioned phonograph. Wide-eyed watchers in the booth noticed for the first time that his makeup had been daubed on with slap-dash abandon, showing waxy white patches of skin, and his lips moved with a strange mechanical stiffness.

"At left tackle," he repeated, fumbling and groping for words that would not come, "at left tackle, ah, Bob, ah . . ."

The cameraman stared at the cable man. Spotters jabbed frantic fingers at the charts in front of him. The floor man stared helplessly at Ray Scott, who was to assist Stern in the broadcast. Billy Whitehouse, ABC's sports editor, acted. Snatching up a pencil he scribbled a note and thrust it in front of Stern.

"Give it to Scott."

Bill Stern did. Then he sat there, his voice frozen inside him, as the game began. A few minutes later, with painfully studied deliberation, he lifted himself from his chair and stumbled blindly from the booth.

What had happened to Bill Stern?

He wasn't a drinker. ABC, searching desperately for a plausible excuse, announced that he had been shaken up in an automobile accident en route to the stadium.

That was a fantasy, just as were some of the stories Bill Stern had told on the air as he drove himself ruthlessly to success and a $200,000 a year income.

Those entertaining tales which had helped him to fame

had also caused resentment and scorn to be heaped on him, principally by sportswriters demanding the unvarnished truth about their heroes. Bill Stern had walked stony-faced through the storm, apparently unbowed and definitely unyielding, a ready rapier inside a patent leather scabbard. Yet behind that façade there bubbled a mental and physical volcano.

When one sportswriter heard that Bill Stern's life story was being written, he asked bluntly, "Who's publishing it, Hans Christian Andersen?"

But this is no fairy tale.

It is the story of a comeback, surpassing in credibility any of the inspired and doctored tales which made Bill Stern famous on the air. It is a story of shocking disclosures—of smoldering resentment, personal tragedy, physical agony, and mental torment. How Bill Stern fought through sixteen tortured years for peace, health, and happiness and emerged with a new-found faith and gentleness is a saga of inspiration and hope.

Bill Stern blames his troubles on no one but himself.

The golden, flowing voice which once turned to stuttering brass is vibrant and strong again. Firmly it analyzes the Bill Stern of old: "I was a coward."

What really happened to Bill Stern is told here for the first time. The patience and love of many others helped him in his painful climb from terrible depths to wholesome heights he never before had been able to attain. Yet it couldn't have been accomplished except for his own fortitude and tenacity.

This is Bill Stern's story. And, when you know it, you also will know that if Bill Stern was a coward he stands forth proudly today as the most courageous coward any of us ever has been privileged to know.

—Oscar Fraley

Chapter 1

There it o'ertook me that I fell down for thirst, I was parched, my throat burned, and I said: "This is the taste of death."

—The Story of Sinuke, ancient Egypt

HARRIET STOPPED THE CAR for a traffic light, and breaking a long silence pointed ahead to the opposite corner. "There it is, Bill."

I hugged my arms across my stomach. There was a swelling, icy knot inside and yet a trickle of sweat ran down my forehead. I didn't dare wipe it away. If I moved my arms the iceberg in my middle might get larger.

"Yes," I agreed, trying to keep my voice level. "Yes, there it is."

Neither of us said anything else as the car slid ahead. My eyes followed the high, forbidding brick wall until we slowed at the gates to a driveway. A cold bronze sign stared out at me. The block letters marched out their message impersonally.

"Institute Of Living."

My wife turned the car in under the big elm trees and all I could think of was that this was to be my prison. Once again, wooden-faced, uncaring strangers were going to "make me well." Or try.

I was scared. I had been through this before. Not here but in other places.

First there would be a few days of pure, unadulterated hell. There would be interminable hours which I counted off in faltering seconds, with the relentless sensations of intense anxiety and extreme nervousness. Unexpected sounds would make me jump like a marionette with tangled strings and I would have to grit my teeth to keep from screaming. Then I would.

After that it hits you in the stomach. Your intestines gurgle and growl. Nausea rams an iron fist against your abdomen and your heart throbs with such thunderous beats that you are certain it can be heard across the room.

Then you perspire, as I was doing now while Harriet headed the car across the courtyard and toward a circular driveway which led up to a central building, wooden-faced and with blank-eyed windows. The drops roll down your temples in rivers of agony and from under your arms they burn a pathway over your ribs.

Your nose runs. You yawn endlessly. Then you have chills. Your teeth chatter and your arms jerk spasmodically no matter how hard you try to keep them still. You ache, in bone-deep stabs. The hot flashes come back to be replaced almost immediately by those icy chills.

Then it gets worse.

The ends of every nerve in your body are livid and burning, as mine were beginning to be now as Harriet swung the car in front of the steps leading to a pair of double doors.

What was beyond them, I wondered? Not that it much mattered.

After the first few excrutiating days, I knew from experience, it wouldn't be too bad. The nightmare would slack off and there was no reason why this day of June 16, 1956, should be any different than other such days in other years.

They'd straighten me out, objectively and for a price. They'd get me back on my feet and in a few days, or a few weeks at most, I'd be back home with Harriet and ready to face the world all over again. It wouldn't take long, or, for that matter, last long.

Or would it?

Maybe this really was the end of the road for Bill Stern. How much can a man take? Maybe even more important, how much can a woman take? And Harriet had said just that; said it with steely finality.

As the car stopped, I could see her again sitting in our living room, biting her nails, twisting a handkerchief, tears welling up in those blue eyes which once had been so full of laughter. Her voice this time held no compromise.

"Bill, I can't, no, I won't, take this any longer. This thing has driven me to the point where you must do something about it, once and for all, or I am going to leave you."

There had been much more; recriminations, pleading, and hours of tear-stained discussion before, at last, we decided that I should go to Hartford for an indefinite stay.

There had been an alternative. But it was too close to home. This time it had to be done, more or less, on my own. I had to want it desperately enough to make it stick. This couldn't be merely another weak effort, a few weeks of uneasy peace and then a gradual slide back into the same dark depths.

But could I do it?

That question nagged me all the way up the Merritt Parkway. Harriet drove silently, relieved to be busy with the wheel. Actually there was little to say, nothing more left to be said. Traffic was light and it was a warm, pleasant day, yet my thoughts blotted out the freshness of the foliage and the blue beauty of the sky overhead.

I had taken Demerol to get me to Hartford without any unnecessary anguish. It calmed my nerves and in the beginning I wasn't too apprehensive. But as the miles and the Demerol wore away, I began to get more and more uncomfortable. The old questions which seemed to have no permanent answers taunted me and I was becoming increasingly tense and irritable as we neared our destination.

What had brought me here and to this state?

It seemed to me to have started twenty years earlier when, on a bright, sunny morning in Texas, I drove headlong into another automobile. My injuries were severe but should not have been critical. In the end only sheer criminal medical neglect resulted in amputation of a left leg which had suffered a compound fracture but should have been saved. Ever since, the merciless nerve ends in the stump had contributed their bit, periodically turning through some diabolic witchery into twitching tentacles of fire.

Then there had been the kidney stones; many real, more imagined. They had paved my path to innumerable hospitals and obliging doctors for the surcease brought by the needle.

Frustrations and rejections also had conspired to reinforce my craving for the nerve-soothing solace and confidence produced by sleeping pills, seconal, codeine, Demerol, Dilaudid, or the morphine syringe.

"Coward, coward," I shouted silently to myself, as Harriet parked the car and I looked bitterly up the steps to those forbidding doors. "If you hadn't been such a coward you wouldn't have let a little pain get you down."

Life for me in those past sixteen years had been a restless elevator raising and lowering me endlessly between injected heights and depressing depths.

There had been many rewards, I had to admit. I had a devoted wife and three fine children. Money was no problem, because I had earned large sums and saved systematically. I drove myself to do this, always remembering in the back of my mind the pitiful, impoverished man my father had become after his wealth had been blown away in the stock market crash of 1929.

Somewhere I had lost the road. Now I had to find it alone or become, through days which would be limited, forever a wanderer.

Harriet had left me no doubt about that—which was understandable even in my state. How much, I asked myself, can one human being expect another to withstand? Faithfully she had stood beside me through all these years, her love and her support and, somehow, even her belief in me, never wavering even after that Texas accident which preceded our wedding.

The glory of it had rubbed thin with the rush of the years. I had lived at a frantic pace, seeing much more of the inside of trains, planes, and hotel rooms than of Harriet and the children. Ruefully I remembered the time she had pasted my picture over Peter's crib and her quiet remark, half joking, half serious, "Just so he'll know what his daddy looks like."

A fine picture now, I thought bitterly, as we sat there silently in the car, neither wanting to make the first move.

This trip, so brutally necessary, had started for me six months earlier on a bright day in New Orleans, which was one of the darkest I shall ever know. I was to broadcast the Sugar Bowl game, the same game which had been my first bowl assignment back in my early radio days of 1937 and which Harriet and I went to again so joyfully on January 1, 1938.

But the game on New Year's Day, 1956, was a blight on my memory. I had come apart at the seams.

The months between that fiasco and these miserable moments, as we sat in the car while I worked up courage to get out and climb those waiting stairs, had been a nightmare.

The voice of which I had always been so proud had become cracked and hesitant. Forming words was an almost impossible chore and my mind was reluctant to accept the challenge. I had arrived at a state where I could neither rest nor read, eat nor sleep, concentrate nor care.

I was, I knew full well, a trembling, putty-skinned caricature whose path had disappeared in a wasteland of nowhere.

My thoughts were interrupted as Harriet, her hands white-knuckled on the steering wheel, cleared her throat. I realized she had been staring at me speculatively while she waited.

Her voice was low, but it reached out to give me strength. "Well, Bill, we might as well go in."

I nodded, wearily reluctant. "Yes, we might as well."

Pushing the car door open slowly, I realized that I was soaking wet with nervous perspiration. My heart was pounding apprehensively, booming so loudly in my ears that I was sure Harriet must hear it. I looked at her, but she merely waited at the foot of the steps, her face expressionless.

Slowly, as a man sleepwalking, I clambered from the car. Softly and with great reluctance, I shut the door behind me. Then, one by one, Harriet moving beside me like a shadow, I climbed the steps until we stood silently at the top.

My hand reached out mechanically and fastened on the

doorknob. I looked down at it as if it belonged to someone else and for an instant closed my eyes as all of the old fears, doubts, and anxieties crowded in around me.

"Oh, God," I groaned through locked teeth, "why has this happened to me? What has brought me here?"

Then I opened the door and went inside.

Chapter 2

Of all the animals, the boy is the most unmanageable.
—Plato

LIFE BEGAN FOR ME in Rochester, New York, on July 1, 1907, and my earliest memories are of a roomy, pleasant red brick house where, it seems, we always had more than we could ever need or want.

In retrospect I would have to admit that my brother, Tom, three years my elder, and I both had too many material things. If there was anything we lacked it was the close-knit family association which brings deep love and understanding and provides the sense of well-being and fullness so necessary to conquer childhood's fears and mold rock-solid character.

My father, Isaac Stern, was a tall, powerful man with vivid red hair, a bluff, hearty manner, and a lively sense of humor. He was inordinately proud of his two sons and he spoiled us completely when it came to material things. On the other hand, as head of Michaels-Stern, the third largest manufacturer of men's clothes in the world, he was too busy to spend much time with us. He compensated for this in his own mind by giving us everything we wanted.

Mother, who had been Lena Reis of a well-to-do Cincinnati family, was the balancing factor. She was tall and slender but, as I look back, she never seemed completely happy. With us boys she was kind but not demonstrative. Firm in her desire to give us a solid upbringing, she would have no compromise. To her things were black or white, right or wrong, and there was no in-between.

When I was eight years old we moved to East Avenue, the "Park Avenue" of Rochester, where my father had built an enormous white colonial-type house complete with six bedrooms, patio, sun porch, screened sleeping porch, butler's pantry, and servants' quarters. It was here, when I was ten, that I made the house ring with my new saxophone and became, I thought proudly, quite proficient.

Here, too, when I was eleven, stealthily I removed the hinges from the locked garage door, backed out our Pierce Arrow, and drove up and down East Avenue until the red-faced chauffeur collared me. Mother insisted that I be punished. Father merely laughed.

My boyhood on the whole, I suppose, was much like any other in a home of material plenty. Yet as I moved into my teens and became more and more socially conscious there was a difference which made a deep impression on me. We were Jewish. As I arrived at an age where "belonging" meant a great deal, for the first time I felt the stab of prejudice. Rochester was a city with an "upper class" social whirl. Because of my father's excellent standing in the community we were usually a gladly accepted part, but I was bitterly hurt when, on occasion, I was excluded from one of the party lists, isolated with other members of my faith. Life at these moments hinted at all the miseries it could hold.

Meanwhile, I attended the Rochester public schools and, it must be added, without distinction. There were just too many other things to do. At fifteen I was certain that I was one of the world's greatest saxophone players. Looking back, I know I didn't actually play well but I must confess I played loudly. Eventually I assembled an orchestra which I was convinced was the world's best but which undoubtedly was an atrocity on the world of music. This combo I proudly called "Bill Stern and his Bluegrass Music."

With brassy self-assurance and using my father's name without permission, I inveigled a Rochester theater to engage my band. Needless to say, we made little money. The salaries for my orchestra totaled about three hundred dollars for the week but I was paid only one hundred dollars for the entire group. There was nothing else but for Father to bail me out by making up the two hundred dollar deficit. Yet the feeling which it gave me, standing up there on the stage as the center of attraction, was so stimulating that I booked us into the theater again at Christmas vacation. We repeated the process of making bad music and losing money. Once again Father rescued me without a murmur.

After my first year in high school even Father was aware that I needed a stronger restraining hand, and after due deliberation I was packed off to Hackley Preparatory School in Tarrytown, New York.

There I did so well that I was placed on probation during my first year and warned that unless I mended my ways I would be kicked out the next year.

I was.

The reason was that, even at this early age, I had an irresistible compulsion to "be somebody." I was crazy for

Broadway, the bright lights, and band music. I read *Variety* as fast as they could print it. And, always having more than enough spending money from Father, I skinned out for New York at every opportunity.

It was easy. Outside my window at Hackley was a substantial drainpipe. It was no chore to dress carefully after lights out, shinny down the drainpipe, and take a train to New York. On one of my early trips I met a pert, dark-haired young dancer named Rubye Stevens at the Strand Roof. I was smitten completely, even though Rubye considered me merely a friend. I felt a sense of great personal triumph when she obtained a part in a Broadway show called *Keep Cool.* Subsequently she changed her name to Barbara Stanwyck.

But there was nothing cool about my reception from the school authorities when, after several warnings, they caught me climbing back up the drainpipe in the wee hours of the morning. There was another warm reception at home after I was expelled.

Mother cried at the shame I had brought to the family.

The following year I was sent off to Cascadilla Prep in Ithaca, New York. This, too, as chance would have it, was a poor choice. Cascadilla was about to go out of existence and the teachers, knowing that they were not to be retained, were not inclined to be too demanding. I spent the whole year avoiding classes without being tossed out merely because no one else was doing much except wasting time.

At the end of the year I compiled the unenviable record of flunking fifteen college boards in an effort to enter Cornell University.

But by this time I had become proficient enough at the saxophone to get a job with a band at Breeze Inn, a dime-a-dance palace outside Ithaca, where I stayed through the summer on the pretense of boning up for the Cornell entrance examinations which I already had failed. Also during that summer my parents went off to Europe and I fell in love.

She was a lovely, blue-eyed blonde named Evelyn Rapalee, and while it was a virginal and innocent affair it marked the first time I was ever serious about a member of the opposite sex. Although I was only seventeen we talked blissfully of marriage, and merely having someone who returned my affection filled a need deep within me. For this I remember Evelyn gratefully and fondly, even though as I went on to college we drifted apart and she eventually married someone else.

That summer, too, as an illustration of what an exemplary young man I was, I made several trips home while my parents were abroad. It was during prohibition and from my father's liquor cellar I appropriated cases of fine eight and ten-year-old Scotch, and returning to Ithaca bootlegged it to my friends for anywhere from thirty-five cents to a dollar a bottle.

That summer, nevertheless, was productive in another way. While my parents were in Europe they had met a young man who was attending Pennsylvania Military College at Chester. Impressed with his poise, manner, and bearing, they decided that P.M.C. was the school for me.

It was one of the best things that ever happened to me. When I entered P.M.C. Prep in 1925 it was driven home rapidly that I could go on for the next five years as I had been and remain a scorned private sweeping out floors, cleaning brass buttons, and shining shoes; or, if I wanted to give the orders and have my buttons cleaned and my shoes shined for me, I could do so with some intensified application. It was a hard lesson, but one which was almost immediately obvious, even to me.

Thus at P.M.C. I began to work for the first time in my life.

There were other factors which influenced me. Instead of allowing me to feel sorry for myself and bemoan the fact that it was a very strict school they taught me swiftly that everybody else was in exactly the same circumstance. There were no favorites. This was a military school. There was no room or reason to sulk, pout, or cry. Each cadet had it just as rugged as the next one. For the first time Iasac Stern's money meant absolutely nothing in the life of young Bill Stern.

Up to now father's money always had been able to buy me special favors. Here it was useless. There was only one recourse and I took it. I began to study and, for the first time in my adolescent life, began to get fairly good grades. I began to learn, also, to control a quick, almost ungovernable temper, although this took somewhat more doing.

The first crack in my arrogant armor came after I made the polo team. One day during a practice session something went wrong and I burst into a string of polished profanity associated with much more hardened cavalrymen.

"Mr. Stern," the coach reprimanded me, "polo is a gentleman's game. You, sir, will turn in your equipment."

But I did make the P.M.C. Prep football team as a halfback and, to a boy who had failed to stick on the squad at Hackley and who had rowed for an indifferent team at Cascadilla, this was a colossal morale boost. I still recall the thrill of running some fifty yards for a touchdown, which, incidentally, was the only touchdown I ever scored.

Finally I belonged. It was a great feeling. No longer did I worry merely about passing. Now I was determined to advance from the ranks, from private to corporal, from corporal to sergeant, from sergeant to lieutenant. For the first time I was truly applying myself. Proof of how well I learned to do so was that in my senior college year I was appointed captain adjutant on merit alone, and I was graduated second in my class.

The academic drive which I had acquired and my duties as an officer precluded my playing football as a senior, but I did play quarterback in a junior year in which our efforts are memorable only because of their futility.

I was such a sterling quarterback that we lost every game and one of my most vivid recollections is of picking up the nickname "One-Yard Kelly." My teammates dubbed me thus because of the hair-trigger temper which I struggled not too successfully to control—evolving the quip that "he must be a fighting Irishman"—and the distressing fact that one yard usually was the extent of my advance when carrying the ball.

To further clinch my case as strictly not one of All-America caliber, we wound up the year playing Albright, a team which also had not won a single game.

"This is one game we're sure to win," we boasted.

When the final gun sounded we bowed our heads in shame at the drubbing Albright administered to us. They had won, 40 to 0.

But, while I was far from being a success as a quarterback, I was discovering, cliché or not, that you get out of life exactly what you put into it.

P.M.C. changed me immeasurably from the careless, irresponsible boy who had imagined he could buy his way through life. The reformation was not complete, possibly, but it was a flying start in the proper direction, and if subsequently life reflected turbulence it was not because of a lack of proper training in those early years at P.M.C.

No one can contend that this progress extended to my music, even though I led the college orchestra at P.M.C. almost from the time I reached college level. I was far from being an accomplished saxophonist, but what I lacked in quality I made up in quantity—I owned a baritone sax, an alto sax, a C-melody sax, a soprano sax, and a clarinet. And, while my chief forte was enthusiasm and volume, this awesome display of instruments convinced my schoolmates that I must be the proper man to lead the group.

My brother, Tom, was married in 1927 to Amy Heilbroner, a daughter of Louis Heilbroner of the Weber and Heilbroner clothing chain in New York. There was an elaborate reception at the Ritz Carlton Hotel at which Meyer Davis, the society orchestra leader, furnished the music. On impulse I sat in with the band when it rendered "Somebody Stole My Gal," the one number I could perform with professional skill. This so impressed another collegian at the wedding that he invited me to join an orchestra he was forming for a trip to Europe the following summer.

I agreed, and on a June morning in 1928 our combo arrived at the dock to board the French liner S.S. *DeGrasse*. Our hopes were almost annihilated. The purser had never heard of us. The fly-by-night booking agent we had engaged had taken the $250 advance we paid him to line up the job, told us we had it, and vanished. After much discussion we finally effected an agreement with the purser and were taken aboard.

There were six of us and the only sleeping space available was in the contagious disease ward. We took it happily and sailed antiseptically off for Europe. The purser, however, soon discovered that he had made a poor bargain.

The first night we played for the first-class passengers. At their request, the second night we played for the second-class passengers. At their request, the third night we played for those in third-class. At everybody's request, from the fourth night on we merely relaxed and enjoyed our trip to Europe.

We were in trouble again on our arrival in Paris, where

we learned that the booking agent also had failed to obtain the promised engagement. We were unemployed and fast running out of funds when we heard that Fred Waring, the American orchestra leader, was performing at a restaurant on the Champs Elysées. We went to him, and after listening to our plaintive tale he engaged us to augment his orchestra.

We must have been very trying because whenever Waring wanted to play a particularly melodious arrangement he raised a finger to his lips and our group, only pretending to play, went through the motions silently. It was only Waring's kindness which enabled us to eat while we were making transportation plans to get back to the United States.

Father had been against my making this trip, and while I knew he would send me the money if I asked for it my new training came to the fore and I determined to solve my own problem.

I did, shoveling my way home on a cattle boat while my fellow bandsmen made various other arrangements.

Eagerly I looked forward to my return to P.M.C., but while I was gradually learning how to work there still was no great necessity driving me forward. Going into my final year, in September of 1929, I was not saddled by the anxieties which face most young men preparing to leave their school years behind them and plunge into the business of making a living.

Money never had been a problem. We always had servants, as many as two chauffeurs at a time and two or three new automobiles in the garage. I had my own convertible, and the future seemed very promising now that I had, as I thought, accepted the facts of life.

Father made another trip to Europe where he met an expert on branch banking, and upon his return home invested almost his entire capital in Trans-America stock.

Then came the stock market crash in October, 1929, and

the stock plunged from seventy to seven. Father was wiped out in a winter of desperate financial maneuvering.

As the depression clamped down it grasped me, along with millions of others, in its iron fingers. As I neared graduation from P.M.C., instead of being a young man with no financial worries, I was faced with the heretofore unconsidered task of making my way alone and unaided.

It was then that I decided if I ever had money of my own I would never invest it in the speculative stock market. It is a decision which I have followed faithfully. The stocks I own have been purchased purely for their dividend value.

My father's misfortune left its mark and when I graduated from P.M.C. in June, 1930, I was a much sobered and somewhat frightened young man.

Father, reeling under his setbacks, still attempted to provide all he could materially. He had clung to a new Pierce Arrow touring car and despite his dwindling funds he had the car converted into a handsome runabout, which he presented to me as a graduation gift.

Chapter 3

Fame is the thirst of youth.
—Lord Byron

I ACQUIRED A GREAT DEAL at P.M.C. in addition to formal education, gaining a certain amount of poise, polish, and assurance almost as much by sheer osmosis as through an expanding willingness to apply myself. And yet it was to require a postgraduate tutoring by time before I could perceive that life had much, much more to teach me.

Youthful exuberance fenced off immediate awareness of the problems I faced in my transition from a life of plenty.

Although I no longer received those comforting checks from home which I had always accepted as a matter of course, I was armed with the brash, resilient confidence of youth. After all, I was the late captain adjutant, a musician of sorts, and quite satisfied with my talents and appearance. I owned a new automobile, and inspired by my ceaseless reading of *Variety* through the years I decided to go to Hollywood and become a rich and famous actor.

Thus I teamed up with a classmate named Carl Class and we set forth enthusiastically for the motion picture capital to permit fortune to tap lightly and effortlessly on our shoulders.

Even the dirt roads in Arizona and New Mexico contributed to the lark which we made of that week-long journey. Once there we rented a room in a boardinghouse and began a gay tour of the movie lots, along with such side trips as visits to the Agua Caliente race track. With such a mode of living our money didn't last long.

Another who was finding life to be not exactly the joy ride we all had envisioned was a young man with whom we became friendly—Arthur Rothafel, son of the famed Sam Rothafel, known to the entertainment world as Roxy. We were commiserating with each other over a bottle when Arthur snapped his fingers suddenly and grinned, "I've got it. We'll send my father a telegram."

It was a beaut. Addressed to him at the Roxy Theater in New York it had all the finesse of a sledge hammer. I can see it now:

Boy believed to be your son found in a dead faint on boardinghouse floor. Suggest send money as he is suffering from malnutrition.

Bill Stern, a friend.

Roxy was horrified and acted instantaneously. But instead of sending the ready cash we had anticipated, he telephoned immediately to Erno Rapee, director at the Roxy who happened to be in Hollywood writing the score for *Seventh Heaven*. Rapee dropped everything for a race to the boardinghouse, where he burst in on three startled fellows suffering not from malnutrition but from being slightly high on cheap rye whisky.

Rapee really laid us out before telephoning Roxy that his son was all right. Meanwhile, Mrs. Rothafel, in a state of great agitation, had thrown a few clothes into a suitcase and, accompanied by her daughter, Beta, had left on the moment for California to rescue Arthur and bring him home. When she arrived in Hollywood and learned it was all a frightful hoax, her relief was so great that she forgave all of us. But Mrs. Rothafel's reactions made little impression on me, for I was too occupied staring at blond, blue-eyed Beta. I was in love again, and under Beta's inspiration I immediately went out and obtained a job with RKO.

I dug postholes for five dollars a day.

This wasn't exactly getting me in front of the motion picture cameras and after three days of blisters and backaches, topped off despairingly by the return of Mrs. Rothafel and a reluctant Beta to New York, I decided to quit and follow them.

When I arrived in the East, there was nothing to do but go home to Rochester and there in September I obtained a job with Michaels-Stern. It was a very important job—I pushed tacks into a map. A white tack meant one kind of store and a red tack meant another, and I had such a fumbling thumb that they soon moved me into the pants pressing department. There again I was such a distinct failure that after a brief period I was transferred to the cutting department, which is just about the last place they could have found for me. My job consisted of raising a lever, inserting a bolt of cloth, and lowering the lever to cut the cloth along designated lines. Even so, I managed to ruin more than one bolt of cloth.

In the meantime I was corresponding steadily with Beta, frustrated that our romance was on a siding, with her in New

York and me in Rochester. Finally, by letter and telephone I prevailed upon her to bring her parents to Rochester so that my family could meet them. We hoped that possibly they might permit us to announce our engagement.

Roxy at this time was one of the brightest stars in the entertainment industry, the Flo Ziegfeld, Cecil B. De Mille, and Mike Todd of the era. Theatrical impresario, with a theater named after him, he had opened and operated most of the important theaters on Broadway and had introduced many stars in his shows. Naturally, his arrival in Rochester was heralded with fanfare.

Father was so impressed he even scraped together enough money to have the inside of the house redecorated, though in those days of the Depression he could ill afford such extravagance.

Our plan came off successfully, and after the Rothafels arrived, Beta and I were permitted to announce our engagement. Roxy refused to give me a job, however, firmly suggesting that I remain in Rochester rather than try to crash the rugged entertainment world in New York.

I saw nothing for me to do but prove him wrong, so I quit my job with Michaels-Stern and went to New York. There, after much pavement pounding, I got a job in January, 1931, as an usher at a theater called the Japanese Gardens. My salary was eleven dollars a week. When Roxy heard about this from Beta he exploded and then, after his blood pressure settled back to normal, told her, "Well, if he's going to be an usher, he might as well be one for me. Tell him to come down to the Roxy."

So I went to work at the Roxy for sixteen dollars a week and learned to know and admire the man who remains a legend of show business. Roxy was a strict disciplinarian but a magnificent showman with a vivid imagination, wonderful taste, and an infallible feeling for what the public wanted.

I was an usher for about three weeks only. During this time, after the last show ended I would slip surreptitiously into the rear of the theater and watch throughout the night as new shows were put through dress rehearsals. I did this out of honest interest and without attempting to influence Roxy—they were simply magic moments I didn't want to miss—yet I was conscious that Roxy knew I was there. Observing my unflagging enthusiasm, and, I am quite certain, wishing to help his future son-in-law, he directed Leon Leonidoff, the producer, to give me a job backstage. Leonidoff had no job but he created one and I became assistant to the assistant stage manager at thirty dollars a week.

"Just remember one thing," Roxy warned me. "Keep your eyes open and your mouth shut."

I learned quickly. I just nodded.

I learned other things quickly, too. I had only been on the job about three months when, while Roxy was in Europe scouting for new talent, the stage manager resigned and the assistant stage manager announced that he also was leaving. Seeing that there was no one on the present staff who could take over as stage manager, I rushed to Leonidoff.

"Leon," I asked breathlessly, "can I have the job?"

Leonidoff, a short, excitable man who spoke a language all his own, laughed gustily and turned me down flat. The essence of his refusal was that I lacked experience, which was certainly true.

Whereupon I did something that later was to be fairly typical of my career. I went over Leonidoff's head and cabled Roxy in Russia.

`Stage manager and assistant leaving. May I have job and salary?`

Roxy's reply consisted of one word.

Yes.

I don't believe that even in my wildest dreams I imagined he would give his consent. I thought perhaps I might become assistant stage manager. But Roxy was so nonplused by the audacity of my cable that he thought if I felt I was ready for the job he was willing to take a chance. Then, too, he knew Leonidoff was always on hand to step in if necessary.

The excitable Leonidoff, a gifted and brilliant man, hit the ceiling when I told him what I had done and what Roxy had replied. He grew red in the face, he bellowed, he roared. But there was nothing else he could do except give me the job. And with it my salary jumped from thirty dollars to one hundred fifty dollars a week. Now I really worked and tried desperately to do a job which, barring a few crises, I managed well enough.

Sometime after Roxy's return from Europe he realized an ambition which had been his dream—plans were completed to build Radio City. This ambitious project embodied the ideas of three men: Roxy, utilities magnate Owen D. Young, and "Deac" Aylesworth, president of the National Broadcasting Company. It was to be exactly what the name implied, a city of radio. It was to house NBC and two theaters, the Music Hall and the Center. Plans called for the Music Hall to open with two-a-day showings and the Center Theater was designed originally to house the Metropolitan Opera Company.

Roxy thereupon resigned from the Roxy Theater and took with him his entire staff. This included Erno Rapee, the musical director I had met under such strange circumstances in Hollywood; Leonidoff as producer; Florence Rogge, ballet director; Russel Markert, in charge of the Roxyettes who later became the Rockettes; Vincente Minnelli, a great Hollywood director once married to Judy Garland, in charge of scenery.

And Bill Stern, stage manager.

We were given office space in the Palace Theater Building, owned by RKO, which was to sponsor the Music Hall, and we all took a hand in assisting Roxy to lay out the Radio City Music Hall. Meanwhile, we also were put to work in other theaters. I worked, from time to time, in the Academy of Music and at the Palace before being called to work exclusively on the stage of the Music Hall.

The dreaming and planning finally came to fulfillment in December, 1932, when we opened, actually without having had a complete dress rehearsal. It was a fiasco.

The stage was not ready until a month before the opening and there never had been anything in the business to compare with its gigantic complexity. The result was that everything was hooked up backward.

When Roxy asked that the stage be revolved, I would push the "revolve" button and the stage, with Erno Rapee and some hundred surprised musicians, would rise into view. When he asked that Rapee and his hundred musicians be made to disappear, I would press the "down" button and up would come the steam curtain. The button to remove the curtain brought the ballet into view. As I said, everything was topsy-turvy.

Thus, at the opening of the two-a-day shows, scheduled for afternoon and evening, we had to settle for a debut performance which started finally at nine o'clock at night. By two o'clock in the morning we were only halfway through the second act. The finale of the show was a minstrel number. On rising tiers of the stage, starting at the footlights and going up and back sixty feet to the rear of the stage, some 350 people were seated. These included members of the ballet, the Roxyettes, the glee club, all the extras, the musicians, and the stars. We had never had a dress rehearsal to ascertain whether the machinery actually would lift this manifold number of people and I held my breath as I pushed the button on the trio of elevators which would raise them into view for the finale.

It worked.

But, actually, it didn't matter.

It now was three o'clock in the morning, the weary customers had long since departed, and our first grand finale was played to a house spotted only by a few yawning, die-hard patrons.

Gradually, as the days went by, we worked out the bugs and for a young man of twenty-five it was a pleasurable experience, as well as a great responsibility. I look back on it with satisfaction. I did a good job for a newcomer who had pushed himself possibly too hard and too fast. Still, I had thrown myself into it with extra vigor because, in the spring of 1932, Beta had broken off our engagement.

I hadn't been seeing her too often to begin with. Then, as the job consumed more and more of my time, Beta and her mother went to Bermuda on a vacation and there she met a fine man with whom she fell in love. I was miserably broken up for a time, but gradually the disappointment was erased by my work, new plans, and family difficulties.

The work at the Music Hall was absorbing. Associating with such stars as Weber and Fields, Paul Draper, Jan Peerce, and Martha Graham was a delight to one who always had been starstruck and then I met a beautiful young dancer named Eleanor Powell. Dating her, enjoying her company, and spending weekends at her mother's home in Tuckahoe,

New York, helped me to forget my broken romance with Beta.

Then there were my new plans. The Music Hall was directly across the street from the NBC studios and, after a while, I began to speculate on what it would be like to be a radio announcer. I had never broadcast anything in my life aside from announcing over the public address system at the Music Hall such items as, "Roxyettes on in fifteen minutes" or "Musicians, you have five minutes to get into the pit."

Nevertheless, I began besieging various people at NBC in the hope of getting a break. I met and haunted John Royal, vice president in charge of programming for NBC, and made a constant nuisance of myself.

Throughout this period, family worries also occupied a good deal of my mind. My brother, Tom, who had been injured in 1930 while playing handball, had developed a cancerous growth. Eventually he underwent an operation and, although now money was scarce in our family, in 1933 we sent Tom on a cruise to the West Indies and South America for his health.

I was shocked when I met him at the pier on his return. He was deadly pale and so weak he could hardly stand alone. Tom, the quiet, gentlemanly brother who always had the principles I seemed to lack, was taken immediately to Mt. Sinai Hospital. Within two months he was dead.

It was my first brush with complete disaster. It was not to be my last.

Chapter 4

He was like a cock who thought the sun had risen to hear him crow.

—George Eliot

TWO MONTHS AFTER TOM'S DEATH, when I still was embittered, morose, and melancholy, John Royal lifted me out of my personal depression just as he was to do on a later occasion when I needed him even more desperately.

Life brightened perceptibly when he telephoned in response to my persistent efforts to obtain a radio job and told me that he had decided to let me work with the great Graham McNamee. This was the intoxicating realization of an ambition which up to now had seemed an impossible dream.

What I didn't know was that he figured this was an easy way to get rid of me. Privately he told McNamee, "Take this fellow Stern with you when you do the Navy-William and Mary game at Baltimore and let him hang himself by doing two minutes. Understand, two minutes, and that's all. He has been bothering the life out of me and this will be a good way to get him off my neck."

McNamee in those days was the nation's number one sports announcer, the first national radio idol in this field. He proved to me that day that he was one of the finest men I was ever to be privileged to know.

Graham kept me beside him throughout a colorless ball game without letting me get my eager hands on the microphone. Neither team had so much as threatened to score and I was beginning to despair of getting a chance. But McNamee, in his vast experience, knew that something would give and, what I didn't know, he was saving it for me.

Finally Navy drove down to the William and Mary goal line. There were two minutes to play. This was the first excitement in an otherwise dull game.

McNamee patted my shoulder and handed me the mike.

Navy scored and I looked good telling about it simply because of the excitement being generated down on the field.

My two minutes, carefully selected by McNamee, paid off. John Royal had been listening and when we returned to New York he called me to say that I had surprised him and I would be used again.

He was as good as his word. I did two more games and then Nick Kenny wrote a story about me in the New York *Mirror* which went right to my head. I clipped this very first flattering notice and carried it with me until it was frayed and worn. I bought extra copies. I have it yet, a memento to a monstrously big head. It read:

October 26, 1934

Bill Stern Ace Football Announcer

By Nick Kenny

(Radio Editor, N.Y. *Daily Mirror*)

As far as radio is concerned football is more important

> than the President of the United States. Football is accorded more hours on more stations at any one time than anything else on the air today.
>
> Between the hours of one and six on Saturday afternoons, it is only the very small stations that do not broadcast the actual games. But even they intersperse their Saturday programs with football results. Saturday is football day for radio.
>
> This year's coming ace football announcer, it seems to me, is Bill (NBC) Stern. It is Stern's first year.
>
> Maybe it's because Stern played football with Pennsylvania Military College and was a quarterback that his broadcasts are so interesting. He is interested in what is happening on the gridiron and nothing else. And that's just how the radio fans feel. Stern lets the drama of the game itself hold the emotion of the listeners. He loves the game too well to garnish it with synthetic excitement. Stern really gives you a play by play description of the game. Keep it up, Bill!

I believed every word of it. So much so that, although I had been in the radio business a mere two weeks, I hired myself a manager. This was my first mistake. My manager decided that I was a big property, a big man, and that it was his job to fence me off from the mundane annoyances of a petty world.

He sure did. When John Royal's secretary called me at the Music Hall, where I still was working as stage manager, my personal manager intercepted the call and demanded to know who was calling. Informed that Mr. Royal wanted to talk to me, the manager replied, "Well, you tell Mr. Royal that I am Mr. Stern's agent and any business he wants to do will have to be done through me."

John Royal went right into orbit.

I almost fell through the floor of the Music Hall.

Dashing over to Royal's office, I apologized humbly and

told him that it was a gag pulled by a friend trying to impress outsiders and that certainly I didn't think I was important enough to have an agent.

"Well," Royal observed ominously, "just don't let your head get too big."

So Royal, no longer choleric, gave me an assignment to do one quarter of the Army-Illinois football game to be played that Saturday at Champaign, Illinois.

Relieved as I was to escape Royal's wrath, I still didn't feel that he properly appreciated this new "find" of his. After all, Nick Kenny had praised me highly as an "ace football announcer" and I was certain he was eminently correct. Something would have to be done to impress on Royal how valuable I was.

This was on a Wednesday, and after mulling it over in my mind I hit upon what I thought was a brilliant plan. Thursday morning I got busy on the telephone and called all my relatives, as well as a number of friends, and asked them to send wires to Royal telling him what a superb job I had done on the Army-Illinois game.

There was just one slip between the cup and my big, fat lip. The game, of course, wasn't until two days later. In my naïveté I simply asked them to send the wires without stipulating that they wait until after the game on Saturday.

They sent their glowing messages immediately.

Naturally the telegrams were on Royal's desk Friday morning. And before noon I was summoned to appear in Royal's office "immediately."

Royal, a towering, heavy-set Irishman, was more florid than usual as I walked into his office. And he let me have both barrels.

"You," he growled gruffly, "are really stupid, Stern."

Then, while I shifted from one foot to the other with my mouth dropping wider open every second, he waved a sheaf of telegrams at me and demanded to know how I could have done such a magnificent job on a game which wasn't to be played until tomorrow.

"See this smile on my face?" he grimaced. "Well, it's not in my heart. You, sir, are fired."

My conceit had been my undoing. There was nothing I could say. I walked from Royal's office in a broken-hearted daze.

Of course, I still had my job at the Music Hall. But now more than ever I wanted a career in radio. So as the weeks of that 1934 football season fell from the calendar I trudged more and more helplessly from one studio to another. Without luck. I had done only a few games and all of the other staffs were filled. Nobody would hire me.

When spring came, I finally realized that if I ever was going to amount to anything in radio I would have to work at it full time. Meanwhile, I heard that Stein's Stores, a clothing chain located in the East and the South, was going to sponsor a number of Southern football broadcasts.

So in June, 1935, I took a long gamble and quit my job at the Music Hall. Then I sought out Joe Stein, who was an acquaintance of my father's, and asked him to give me the broadcasting job. Joe agreed and, although it meant working primarily in the clothing business, at least it offered me a chance to return to my beloved radio. This was the end of June, and since I wasn't to start for Stein's until August I decided to take a month's vacation.

When I told my mother of my plans, she suggested that we visit some of our relatives at their summer home in Charlevoix, Michigan. Driving out there from Rochester, at one point during the trip Mother told me, half-ordering and half-pleading, "By the way, you'll meet your cousin, Harriet May, from Grand Rapids. Now, Bill, please remember, I want you to be exceptionally nice to her."

I envisioned my unknown cousin as a pigtailed creature, probably with freckles, buckteeth, and glasses. If I was lucky, I could escort her to one affair and the family duty dictates would be satisfied. I sighed resignedly.

But Harriet when I met her was enchanting. The freckles were there, a thin spattering of golden kisses from the sun dancing across the bridge of her tiny nose. The "buck-toothed" cousin I had imagined was in reality a trim, pert, and vivacious blond with a gamin smile and a bubbling personality.

I had been surrounded by beautiful women for more than four years at the Music Hall and dated many of them, but Harriet was breath-taking and by far more exquisite than anyone I had ever seen on the stage.

I soon learned, too, that she not only was beautiful but also possessed a quick, level-headed intelligence. A student at the University of Michigan, she was besieged by a swarm of suitors but I took full advantage of the fact that I was "one of the family" and allowed her no time for others.

We swam, danced, and picnicked. We walked hand-in-hand. We were constantly together. I was more content than I ever had been in my life. At last I had found someone with every quality I deemed desirable, and the nagging loneliness I had known vanished completely. In little more than a week, stumbling and halting like a schoolboy, I told her how I felt about her and she agreed to date no one else and to be "my girl."

I was irrevocably in love and this time I knew beyond doubt that it was the real thing.

There were obstacles, of course. I was twenty-eight, Harriet was only nineteen, and her father, in addition to wanting her to finish college, didn't particularly approve of me. By the same token he didn't approve of anybody else simply because, like most fathers, he didn't think anyone was good enough for her.

Nor did my mother approve of our plans as we began to discuss marriage, although she found no objection in the fact that we were cousins. While at the Music Hall I had flitted from one affair to another as any young bachelor "on the town" in New York might. Then there had been the broken engagement with Beta Rothafel which, along with my various escapades since boyhood, convinced Mother that I was too wild to ever settle down.

Harriet and I knew, however, against all objections, that we wanted to belong to each other.

Yet, even as we discussed marriage, it was Harriet who was the sensible one, sensible and understanding. I would have plunged in, come what may. Gently, persuasively, and with a loving tenderness surprising in one so young, Harriet curbed my impatience.

"Let's give ourselves a bit more time while I finish college," she soothed. "We know what we want, Bill, and it will work itself out. If we wait a bit, we'll be more certain than ever that this is the right thing we are planning. Being separated for a short time will give both of us time to make sure of our minds and our love. It is the right thing, I am sure."

I chafed at this enforced delay, but as the days went by I accepted her decision, adored this slip of a girl more than ever, and contented myself with our engagement until I could crack the radio field. When the day came for Mother and me to leave Charlevoix, Harriet arose at 5:00 A.M. to see us off, and we promised each other that nothing would come between us. This time, I vowed to myself, I would not neglect my engagement as I had with Beta Rothafel.

Now I had something else for which to work and I plunged with more determination than ever into the clothing business, an occupation in which I had failed miserably before. Joe Stein assigned me to a store in Schenectady and while possibly I wasn't the best clothing man they ever had, nobody ever tried harder. I pressed pants. I sold suits. I labored diligently in the stockroom. And I waited for a chance to broadcast.

It came, finally, in late September as I listened grimly to others broadcasting the early season games. Joe Stein sent for me and his words were prettier than any music I had ever heard.

"Bill, we have bought sponsorship of the Centenary football games in Shreveport, Louisiana, where we have a store, and you're going to do them for us. I want you to drive down to Shreveport immediately and you'll be there all fall to handle the games."

I was in ecstasy. Thanking Joe profusely, I telephoned Harriet and told her the good news. Then I dipped into my savings and bought a new tan Plymouth convertible. I was going to drive to Shreveport in style. Bill Stern was on his way at last and the networks would learn that they had made a mistake in letting him go.

I didn't feel a single bump all the way to Louisiana. I was riding in the clouds. I was back in radio. And, even though my broadcasting experience at NBC had been rather limited, to say the least, I was greeted and treated in Shreveport as a celebrity. The Stein Stores placed large advertisements in the local newspapers advising the fortunate football fans that Bill Stern, "former NBC network sports announcer," was going to broadcast the Centenary games to them over KWKH, the local station.

It had been arranged that I was to work with Jack Gelzer, KWKH staff announcer, and on October 12, 1935, I returned to the air doing the play-by-play broadcast while Jack filled in the local color. Gelzer was a fine man with whom to work and we formed a competent team. The broadcast went smoothly, and when I returned to the office the Stein executives expressed their hearty approval. I just had to telephone Harriet in long distance celebration.

Life was exhilarating. I had to keep pinching myself to realize that all of this was true. Once again I was back on the air and this time, I determined, nothing would stop me. I'd watch my step and above all that oversized cranium which had cost me my first chance at NBC. This time, I decided, I would let my work speak for itself.

Thus, with a light heart, I set out with Gelzer the following Friday for Austin to broadcast the Centenary game against the University of Texas. It was a beautiful weekend. The weather was ideal and once again the game came off perfectly in both my play-by-play account and Gelzer's color.

I put everything I had into it and when the game was over I leaned back in elated exhaustion. A telephone call from Stein Stores back in Shreveport, complimenting us on the job we had done, made it even more satisfying. Again I telephoned Harriet and then, after an early dinner, went peacefully to bed in my hotel room. My dreams were rosy.

The next day the nightmare began.

Chapter 5

'Tis the wink of an eye,
'tis the draught of a breath,
From the blossom of health
to the paleness of death.
—William Knox

SELDOM HAVE I SEEN a more beautiful, refreshing day than that Sunday morning of October 20, 1935. Well-rested from a good night's sleep and thoroughly pleased with a life which had brought me back into radio broadcasting, I whistled exuberantly while Jack Gelzer and I stowed our bags in my new convertible and headed out of Austin on the way back to Shreveport.

As the city fell behind and the countryside unfolded before us, crisp, clean, and sunwashed, Jack commented continually on the lovely day.

"It's great to be alive," I nodded.

We talked of the game the day before and discussed techniques in broadcasting, as the miles rolled by unnoticed. Now we were on the flatlands of Texas, the prairie stretching out limitlessly on both sides.

In this kind of open driving, speed gradually builds up without realization. The tableland gave no impression of high velocity, and secure in the thought that I could see any approaching or intervening traffic at a great distance I drove relaxed even though my casual glances at the speedometer showed we were doing better than eighty miles an hour.

I'll never know why I hadn't seen it long before I did but suddenly and coming seemingly out of nowhere a car crossed the road directly in front of us. One moment it wasn't there. The next it was squarely in our path as it emerged from a side road.

Automatically I hit the brakes as hard as I could. There wasn't even time to swerve to one side. My tires screamed with a banshee wail and there was a tremendous grinding of metal and shattering of glass as we piled head-on into the side of the other automobile.

The sky and the ground spun, I thought strangely even as darkness closed in around me, much like a pinwheel I had had when I was a child. Screams and the smell of smoke shook me back to consciousness. I was lying in a litter of glass and oil on one side of my overturned car. Somewhere on the other side the car was burning and then, as I tried to rise, I found that both of my legs were pinned under the car.

White-faced and shaking, Gelzer appeared at my side. His quavering voice was almost a shout.

"My God, Bill, I'm not even scratched."

Then he saw that I was pinned down. Putting a shoulder to the wreck, he strained to raise it slightly and somehow I wriggled free. My left leg hung loosely, the foot straying off at an awkward angle, and I knew that it was broken. Jack grabbed me under the armpits and dragged me a safe distance from the burning car.

Then I saw the other car, upside down in the ditch across the road. The screams were coming from inside, and even in my dazed and shocked condition I tried to get up to go to the aid of whoever was inside, only to pitch forward on my face.

I am a bit vague about what happened afterward, for I blacked out again. The next thing I knew, even though we were in the veritable wilderness between Buffalo and Palestine, Texas, several other cars had stopped and a half-dozen men were extricating two people from the car in the ditch across the road.

"We are really lucky," I said to myself as I heard the two people, after gingerly feeling their bodies, gasp that they had escaped without injury. My luck unfortunately, was not to hold.

Meanwhile, among those who had arrived on the scene was a doctor. He took one look at my gashed and twisted leg, and hurriedly opening his bag handed me two small white pills.

"Take these even though we don't have any water," he said. "They'll calm your nerves."

I sat there on the edge of the road, covered with dust and blood and sweating profusely, for more than an hour. Someone, they told me, had driven to a nearby farmhouse to telephone for an ambulance from a hospital in a town called Teague, about twenty miles away.

At first I felt no pain. Then it started, knifing through my leg and lancing up into my thigh in ever-increasing intensity. I sweated even more and bit my lip to keep from crying out.

Eventually, after what seemed like days but actually was about an hour and a half after the crash, an ambulance arrived. Swiftly they hoisted me inside for a jolting, agonized ride over a back road on which every bump was torture. When I thought I could endure no more we stopped and the doors were opened.

"Okay, we're at the hospital," a voice said.

To a boy from the city, it didn't look like any hospital I had ever seen. We were in front of a small, white frame house which, I learned later, was a combination home, doctor's office, and hospital. But the doctor, who directed them to put me on a table in the small operating room, an elderly man but still tall and robust, seemed to me to work efficiently. Within moments an ether cone was clapped over my face and the pain faded away with my consciousness.

Regaining my senses, I found myself in an upstairs bedroom. The leg pained severely and, straining upward, I saw that it had been set in a cast. A few minutes later the doctor appeared.

"You got a compound fracture there, son," he drawled. "But it's all set now and I think everything's going to be all right."

During the night, in which I lay sleepless as the minutes and hours dragged by, the leg became more and more painful. When I called out, a nurse appeared with a hypodermic syringe and gave me an injection.

As the pain-filled days slowly passed, I discovered that all I had to do to obtain relief was to set up a howl. Immediately the soothing needle was forthcoming.

Meanwhile, executives of the Stein store in Shreveport had arrived and I was able to joke about the accident and to realize how fortunate I was to have escaped so lightly. There was a telephone in my room and I called my parents and

Harriet to tell them that there was nothing to worry about. We decided that it was not worth-while for them to come all the way to Texas, because I would be able to leave Teague shortly.

By the third day, however, the pain had become worse. Specialists were summoned from Dallas, and while they couldn't make much of an examination because the leg was in a cast, they probed around to the best of their ability and finally left assuring me that everything apparently was in order.

They were so wrong. The pain mounted until it was one continual wave and I was kept constantly drugged, even though I didn't know it at the time. All I knew was that every few hours the pain would become almost intolerable and I would be given an injection.

At the end of a week it became obvious that something drastic was wrong. The pain was becoming increasingly worse. So finally, after a telephone call to my parents, arrangements were made for me to be put on a train for New York.

The ambulance took me to Palestine, Texas, and there, calmed by another injection, I watched almost in amusement as a window was removed from a sleeping car bedroom and I was hoisted in through the opening. A nurse traveled with me. Her instructions were to make me comfortable, namely with the needle. Dr. Samuel Stein, who took over my case on my arrival in New York, told me later that on this trip I had been given almost enough morphine to kill me. It didn't, and, instead of being in pain, I was in dope-inspired high spirits during most of the trip back to New York.

There was nothing laughable about my condition when I finally arrived and was met by Dr. Stein and my parents.

They were shocked at my drawn, ashen face. Speedily a waiting ambulance took me to the Hospital for Joint Diseases.

Dr. Stein didn't waste any time. No sooner did the ambulance arrive than he began to strip off the cast. Watching the doctor's face, I saw his eyes widen and his lips tighten. Then I was conscious of the odor.

The wound had not been cleansed properly in Texas. From the pus-filled tissue, which now was a festering shade of green, he removed sand, cement, gravel, and even manure which had been rubbed into the leg as I was dragged from the wreck of my car ten days earlier.

Gangrene had set in.

For several days, in that pre-penicillin era, they tried the old method of inserting maggots into the wound to eat away the infection. The leg was too far gone. All this therapy did was make me itch and writhe in pain. When it was almost unbearable, following the pattern established in Texas, they would inject me with morphine. Liberal doses held back the worst of the pain, and while I was becoming progressively worse I didn't really know much about it.

Then came a morning when, without explanation, two orderlies lifted me onto a cart and, joking and talking, wheeled me to the operating room. I had no idea what was going on. Suddenly the doctor bent over me, a gauze mask covering his face, and again the ether cone settled down to sweep me into darkness.

I crawled interminably up a long black tunnel toward a vague light in the distance. It came closer with agonizing slowness and then I was weaving through a heavy white mist. Suddenly, as if a great puff of wind had blown it away, the mist disappeared.

I was back in my room and directly over me Harriet's face seemed to hover, complete in every lovely detail. Struggling as if against a great weight, I reached up in an attempt to caress the softness of her cheek and felt a terrible disappointment as her face disappeared.

Then there was another feeling of singular strangeness which impressed itself on my consciousness. I had no feeling in my leg. Slowly and with great effort I forced myself up on one elbow and my eyes traced the outline of my body under the sheet. Something was queer. The mound under the sheet was too narrow. Then it struck me with the force of a sledge-hammer as I collapsed on my pillow.

My left leg was gone.

It was the greatest shock of my life. Up to this point I had no knowledge that I was to lose the leg. It had never even entered my mind, but now it had been amputated just above the knee. I was horrified.

I was lying there rigidly, in a state of shocked disbelief when Dr. Stein came in, quietly closing the door behind him. He put a consoling hand on my shoulder and his voice was soft and gentle. "I'm sorry, Bill," his words branded themselves into my brain. "We just had to take it off. It was a question of losing the leg or losing your life."

I didn't even answer him. For hours I lay there, alternately cursing and praying, refusing to believe that this had happened to me. I bit my knuckles to keep from screaming, and hammered my fists in frenzied futility against the bed. Gradually I subsided into black despair, filled with a crushing bitterness.

"I would have been better off dead," I told my mother as tears trickled down her cheeks. "I wish I had died on the operating table."

At that time, I meant it. I was inconsolable. I wished a thousand times, ten thousand times, that I would die.

And to make it worse, following the operation the pains

in my legs became even more intense. Now there was the ache of sawed bone and to complicate matters the infection was threatening to spread into the other leg. Now, too, the doctors were becoming concerned about the amounts of morphine I was being given and began to pull back on them. In addition to trying to save my life they now were forced into another battle which could be equally serious.

As they pulled back on the drugs the pain became more and more unbearable. I had heard the word drugs, just like anyone else, but, as to most people, the consequences had little meaning to me. I berated the doctor bitterly.

"You've got to do something to stop this pain," I insisted demandingly. "You've just got to."

After about three days of this, in which the doctor remained adamant and the pain eased infinitesimally, if only because I was becoming more and more accustomed to it, I cared less and less whether I lived. I couldn't sleep and I wouldn't eat and I was going nowhere.

At this point, when I was at my lowest ebb, somebody told John Royal at NBC, the man who had fired me a year earlier, of my condition. Royal came to see me.

He appeared outside my room at about 8 A.M., as the nurse was leaving with a breakfast tray I had not even touched.

"Give me that," the big, bluff Irishman said gruffly to the nurse.

My door swung open and Royal strode into the room and without ceremony thrust the tray onto my lap. His voice was sternly insistent. "How the hell you going to get well and broadcast for NBC if you don't eat?"

He chatted with me as I picked at the food. His booming voice echoed through the room, and as he left, added in an almost embarrassed growl, "When you get out of here and everything's okay, come see me."

It was the best medicine I could have been given. Nor did Royal leave it at that. He sent word to Bill Slater, who was doing the Ohio State-Notre Dame game that weekend, to say over the air that former NBC football announcer Bill Stern was in the hospital and that they were all thinking of me and rooting for me. I cried when I heard that thoughtful message but it gave my morale another much-needed boost.

An amputation is excruciating and soul-searing. Recovery is a long, slow process. My nerves were ragged and there was the added strain of getting over the opiates which had been pumped into me in such frightening quantities. But John Royal had instilled in me once again the will to live.

Royal and Harriet. Every day while I was in the hospital she wrote to me faithfully and tenderly. The first letters I frustratedly tore up. How, I asked myself, could I saddle this lovely girl with a one-legged man, a misfit, a man no longer able to lead a normal life? But still she wrote, unfailingly and encouragingly. Then, hearing of my brightened spirits after Royal's visit, her letters took on a lighter tone until, in one of them, she demanded in one unforgettable line: "Just when are you going to get out of there and marry me?"

She had convinced me that I was important to her life, and Royal hammered home the fact that I still could realize my broadcasting ambitions. It was the twin spur which goaded me back to life.

Ultimately the pains and pangs began to lessen. After six weeks I was discharged from the hospital and returned, weak but on the mend, to an apartment which my family had taken on 88th Street. It was a somber homecoming, for trouble had visited us with a vengeance.

While I was in the hospital my father had suffered a stroke. My brother's death, followed by my accident and loss of the leg, had been too much for him. Mother tried to be cheerful but my condition and that of my father, who had always been hearty and robust but now was confined to bed partially paralyzed, made it a time of suffering and sadness. Within a short time Father was moved to a nursing home. They were painful pilgrimages, struggling on crutches and later hobbling along on my new artificial leg with the aid of a cane, which I made to visit him.

Often I was discouraged to the point of tears. My nerves were as tight as violin strings. The sensitive end of my stump ached and pained constantly and the artificial leg rubbed the tender flesh until it was raw and sore.

My nights were almost unbearable and soon I began to take sleeping pills. In the beginning it was a matter of two or three seconal tablets a night, but even these weren't enough to bring repose. It was a frightful, miserable period of extreme unrest, despair, and constant pain.

Night after night I sat on the side of my bed, staring at the ugly red stump of my leg, and then frantically switching off the light to huddle there untold hours longer staring miserably into the darkness.

Then I would take more sleeping pills, as many as I needed, the number becoming ever larger, to bring me the surcease which came only with sleep.

Chapter 6

Blessed is he who has found his work.
—Thomas Carlyle

IT WASN'T UNTIL the following August, in 1936, that I mastered my artificial leg and my courage enough to go back to NBC. Remembering Royal's words of promise in my hospital room the morning he carried in my breakfast tray, and with the football season coming on, I finally made my way self-consciously to the studios.

Phil Carlin, Royal's assistant, asked me to wait, and then coming back to take me into see Royal he told me confidentially that Royal didn't remember promising me a job.

I talked with Royal a few minutes and thanked him for what he had done for me. Then he picked up the telephone at his elbow and my heart jumped as I heard him say to Carlin, who had returned to his own office, "Stern tells me I promised him a job when he got well, so I guess I did. We'll give him one."

The leg, even in absentia, had done something for me, because plans soon were worked out for me to broadcast football games that fall on an assignment basis. It wasn't a full-time job with NBC but at least it was another much needed start in the right direction.

NBC in those days had the Red and Blue networks. Graham McNamee did most of the games on one network, on which I was to assist him; and on the other were Bill Slater and Don Wilson, later to become even more famous as the Jack Benny announcer. The four of us made up NBC's sports team for the year 1936.

It was good to get back to work and I plunged into it wholeheartedly. I still was connected with the Stein Stores in New York, but the weekends were spent on football. Thus the fall passed swiftly, and I was elated as the season came to an end to be assigned to the Sugar Bowl game at New Orleans, my first Bowl assignment, on New Year's day, 1937.

I had no thought then nineteen years later, at another Sugar Bowl game in New Orleans, the circle would be completed catastrophically.

Broadcasting that first Bowl game was an experience of divided emotions. Being a part of the gala celebration was immensely exciting and yet there was a sadness inside of me, too, because this ended my deal with NBC. Our arrangement had been made for the football season only and there were no plans to take me on as a full-time member of the NBC sports staff.

Returning to New York, I determined not to remain merely a part of a clothing chain's personnel. This determination was strengthened by reunion with Harriet, who had finished school and had come to New York. Although I had faced our reunion with trepidation, happily I found no pity in her eyes, only love and understanding, and I proposed that we get married right away. Once again Harriet was the wiser, agreeing that we should be married but that first I should make one last all-out effort to obtain a full-time radio job. Harriet made the decision and set the date.

"Take your time, Bill, and look around until you have exactly what you want. Let's say we'll get married at the end of April. That will give you a good two months to decide what you want to do. But, no matter what it is, I'm with you all the way."

I was cheered and comforted. And now that I was about to take a wife I redoubled my efforts to get a steady radio job.

Through the grapevine I heard that Mike Cowles, a friend of mine who owned several radio stations in Iowa, was looking for an announcer. He then was in Des Moines so I took a trip out there to see him, and Mike, who today is publisher of *Look* magazine, offered me a full-time radio job at a salary of seventy-five dollars a week.

Elatedly I telephoned Harriet the news and a mutual friend found us a house in Des Moines in which Harriet and I expected to start housekeeping.

Meanwhile, I had returned to New York to resign from the Stein Stores and thankfully leave behind me the clothing business. While I was there I decided to drop in at NBC and thank John Royal and Phil Carlin for all their assistance.

"Well," I told Carlin, "Mike Cowles has given me a job in Des Moines and I won't be pestering you any more because I'm off for the land of the tall corn."

Carlin was surprised and, astonishing to me, appeared concerned. "For goodness sakes, don't do that, Bill," he said.

"If you go out to Des Moines the chances of your ever getting back to New York are mighty slim."

I shrugged my shoulders. "It's a full-time radio job and that's what I'm after."

"Wait a minute," Carlin said with sudden determination. "Let me go in and talk to Royal first."

Carlin hurried from the office and was gone for what seemed an interminable period of time. Then, as I fidgeted and finally got up and was stumping around his office, he returned, a wide smile on his face.

"Royal wants to see you," he grinned.

John Royal was smiling, too. We shook hands and he went right to the point. "Bill, you did a good job for us last fall and, while we don't have a full-time spot for you, we don't want to lose you. So we'll make a spot to keep you here."

He offered me the same salary, seventy-five dollars a week, and I told him that, as much as I appreciated the offer, I would have to get Mike Cowles' permission before I could accept. I had wanted for so long to work for NBC, but now I couldn't in all conscience do it without Mike's approval.

Immediately, I telephoned Mike and told him about the NBC offer and how much I would like to take it unless he objected.

"Go right ahead, Bill," he said cheerfully. "If I had the same choice to make, I'd go with NBC. And the very best of luck to you."

So I started with the National Broadcasting Company on a full-time basis as a sports announcer and a member of the special events department. At last my dream had come true, a dream which had begun in the early 1930's, had been nurtured in 1934 with that original chance to broadcast football, and now had reached culmination. Yet I was to find out quickly how unimportant I was and that I had a long way to go before I could count myself a success.

The "name" announcers in those days were Graham McNamee, Clem McCarthy, Ted Husing, Bill Slater, Jimmy Wallington, George Hicks, Norman Brokenshire, Ben Grauer, and Nelson Case. These were the men writing early radio history and I was a very minor cog in the industry's machinery. I had to be content with working practically unobserved in the news and special events department, keeping busy inconspicuously and doing the best I could, while I waited for my big opportunity.

Harriet and I went ahead with our plans to be married on April 29, and I arranged to take time off for a honeymoon. In the middle of April I received my first outside assignment, the Penn Relays at Philadelphia, after which I was to leave for the wedding.

The Drake Relays at Des Moines were on the same day and a young announcer named "Dutch" Reagan was to handle them from there. NBC would carry both events, switching the network back and forth. Reagan was an extremely pleasant person to work with. When he had an event for which he needed the air I would throw it to him, and when I had an event in Philadelphia for which I needed the air he would throw it back to me.

Reagan was a truly fine sports announcer and although we talked all that afternoon I wasn't to meet him until years later. By that time he had given up sports broadcasting and was Ronald Reagan, motion picture star.

After the relays, Harriet and I were married in New York, on April 29, 1937, and, while it was exceptionally early in the season for a summer resort, we went to Charlevoix where we first had met. There, in a rustic, isolated setting, we spent our honeymoon.

And there, in less than a week, I learned the first lesson which faces every ex-bachelor. An incident occurred which drove home forcefully the fact that I no longer was able to think only of myself. We had been at Charlevoix only a few days when news came that the German zeppelin, the *Hindenburg,* had burst into flames at its mooring at Lakehurst, New Jersey, and had been destroyed with a great loss of life.

"Here I am, off in the Michigan woods, when if I was in New York I'd probably be working on the broadcast from Lakehurst right now," I ranted to Harriet.

Harriet's eyes widened and she burst into tears. I stared at her open-mouthed.

"What's the matter?" I asked dumbfounded.

"That's all you think of our honeymoon," she wept. "You don't care anything about me. All you think of is that darned radio business."

We went fishing.

After our return to New York I continued to work in comparative obscurity for a brief time in the special events department under Abe Schechter, and one of my first outside jobs was to broadcast the America's Cup races at Newport between the British challenger T. O. M. Sopwith's *Endeavor II* and Harold Vanderbilt's *Ranger.*

This is where I was to find out that you never fool around with a microphone.

When we arrived in Newport I was assigned to fly over the races in a plane while Ben Grauer was stationed on a Coast Guard cutter and George Hicks was at a lighthouse vantage point. Coming in on the plane after the first of the best-of-seven races had been completed, I was talking to our engineers, comparing notes over a high frequency transmitter which was not being used for general broadcasting. The chief engineer had all three of us on the wave length, and finally he asked us what we wanted for dinner, telling us that because of the lateness of the hour and the crowded conditions he would put in our orders.

Then, somehow, the conversation lightly turned to the young ladies of Newport and we discussed their charms, thoroughly. It became, to put it mildly, a bit racy.

What we didn't know was that Schechter was on his way to Newport from New York and had our cue channel cut in on the short wave radio in his automobile. He heard it all and blew a gasket because this personal chatter was a violation of Federal Communications Commission regulations and could have cost NBC its license.

That night we were all on our way back to New York so quickly it made our eyes blink. Never was a crew yanked off a job with greater speed.

Abe relented the next day, which happened to be a day off between races anyhow, and we were ordered back to Newport to finish the job. But I, for one, was a very chastened young man with a great deal more respect for the mike than I ever had before.

Another of my early jobs was handling the color for Clem McCarthy in a fight at the Polo Grounds. But in my heart I was only biding my time until the football season arrived, and when it came I was presented with a golden opportunity.

Bill Slater, one of the network's stars, had become involved with John Royal in an argument over Slater's expense account in covering the 1936 Olympic games at Berlin. The expense account was slashed and Bill forthwith told Royal what he could do with it. That ended Slater's decade as a top announcer with NBC. About the same time Graham McNamee was taken off football simply because he was too valuable in other departments. McNamee was doing the

Rudy Vallee program on Thursday nights and the Ed Wynn show on Sundays. If he went on the road for football there was a possibility that he might miss one of these shows, and since they were so important NBC didn't want to take the chance.

This combination of fortunate circumstances moved me right into football's front row and my first staff assignment was to handle the All-Star football game at Chicago that August. At this time, newly married and earning only seventy-five dollars a week, money was scarce and I didn't want to spend more than I had to in making the trip. Therefore, instead of taking the train I figured I'd economize and ride the bus. Which I did, and to my lasting sorrow, because it was one of the most exhausting trips I ever made.

The bus got me into Chicago just a few hours before the kickoff, and coming home I had to take a bus soon after the game ended. My leg still pained me constantly and this bus schedule meant that I couldn't take off my artificial leg from the time I left New York, overnight to Chicago, through the game, and then overnight home again. Even to obtain a few hours of uneasy rest I was still taking sleeping pills almost by the handful.

My pride was piqued, too, on this trip. Feeling very important with my new standing, in chatting to people on the bus I told them that I was going to Chicago to handle the radio broadcast of the game. One fellow, looking at me in disbelief, asked bluntly, "Well, if you're such a big shot, how come you're riding on a bus?"

Coming back I received the same reaction. My traveling companions couldn't believe that I was the one they had heard over the radio. I decided right then that, money or no money, henceforth I would never travel anyway but first-class.

During those early days, although as I have said there was little money in the new Stern household, we were extremely happy. NBC was a fine company with which to work, instilling in its staff members the feeling that they were employed by the best outfit in the business. Then, too, the people with whom I worked as I traveled around the country were friendly and helpful. I have warm memories of men like Pop Warner, Bob Zuppke, Elmer Layden, Clark Shaughnessy, and Frank Thomas. For example, Zuppke, supposedly a hard case, spent most of one whole night instructing me in football formations. They were big names in my business and I was a newcomer, and I remember their help and kindness with fond appreciation.

I was lucky to draw some great games that season. The Yale-Princeton game at Palmer Stadium, which Yale with Clint Frank and Larry Kelley won 26 to 23, still stands out as one of the most thrilling contests I've ever seen. This game, which Fritz Crisler, then the Princeton coach, called "the most exciting game I've ever seen," gave me my first chance to demonstrate what I could do under extreme pressure and excitement. The radio reviews were highly complimentary.

Coming down to the end of that first football season as an NBC staff member, it began to look as if I wouldn't get an opportunity to handle the Army-Navy game, an assignment that I wanted desperately. But there was a feeling in NBC that because the game was so important, they should use their best, namely McNamee. I ardently wanted to do the game and even in those days I still had difficulty controlling that old boyhood temper. Angrily, I told myself that I had handled the top games all season long and now, with a real big one coming up, they had no reason to by-pass me.

But then I remembered from long ago Roxy's advice: "Keep your eyes open and your mouth shut." I did.

I was in Cincinnati, my mother's home town, shortly before the season ended, when I received a wire. When I opened it I was glad immediately that I hadn't made a fuss. The wire was from John Royal.

Because of your fine work, you are going to handle the Army-Navy game.

I was so excited that night that no matter how many sleeping pills I took I couldn't get to sleep. Then, as the season ended, I again was assigned to the Sugar Bowl in New Orleans and this time I took Harriet with me. It was one of our most enjoyable trips together. We dined in the French Quarter, toured Bourbon Street in the gay, noisy hours after dark, and joined in the firecracker-fractured frenzy of the New Year's fiesta.

The following year I began to feel that I had my job well in hand and recognition, slowly but surely, began to come my way. As an example, in 1937 I had finished third to Husing and McCarthy in the poll conducted by *Radio Daily* among newspaper radio editors in every state in the nation. Then, in the 1938 poll, I moved into second place behind Husing.

That season, incidentally, I witnessed the greatest run I've ever seen, before or since, in the Alabama-Tennessee game by a youngster named Johnny Butler. He was trapped four or five times by any number of would-be tacklers but squirmed from their grasp in a weaving dash for a 50-yard touchdown. En route he must have gone 150 yards, plunging and racing from one side of the field to the other and back again. This run has been cut in, over and over again, in feature motion pictures to depict the hero dashing to a spectacular touchdown which wins the game in the last minute of play.

One of my secret ambitions meantime had been to broadcast the Rose Bowl game from Pasadena. There was just one mighty big fly in the ointment. The Rose Bowl, for several years, had refused to use an Eastern announcer on the grounds that we were "too flowery."

This stemmed from an incident involving Graham McNamee when several years earlier NBC first had obtained exclusive Rose Bowl rights, and one in which Graham was an innocent victim. That year, the committee had insisted, as one of the conditions in awarding NBC the game, that since the game was being sponsored by the Pasadena Chamber of Commerce it should provide the pregame copy for McNamee to read, to make certain that Pasadena would be aptly described. NBC agreed.

On the day of the game McNamee was handed his pregame script. It was a perfect description of how Pasadena looked on a beautiful, sunlit afternoon, telling of the azure skies, the purple mountains in the background, and the fleecy white clouds overhead.

Graham had been ordered to read this without fail.

He did.

The only trouble was that it was raining cats and dogs.

McNamee took the rap; a bum one. Newspapers from coast to coast ridiculed him and the committee for the next few years turned thumbs down on Eastern announcers.

But toward the end of the 1938 season, I received another telegram from John Royal. The words bowled me over.

The west coast has changed its mind. They'd like you to handle the Rose Bowl broadcast. Congratulations.

Harriet and I were like a couple of kids. We went to the coast and rubbernecked like all tourists, visiting the studios to gawk as they made motion pictures, dining at famous restaurants without knowing what we ate as we watched for celebrities, and spending New Year's Eve at the Cocoanut Grove.

And we saw one of the most exciting games in Rose Bowl history on January 1, 1939. That was the one in which unbeaten, untied, and unscored upon Duke was leading 3 to 0 going into the final minute of play. Then a fourth string quarterback named Doyle Nave completed four straight passes to a second string end named Al Krueger and Southern California scored with forty-one seconds remaining to play, to win by a score of 7 to 3. When it was over I sat back exhausted.

As I did, Colonel Lemuel Stoopnagle, of the comedy team of Stoopnagle and Budd, came into the booth with a grin on his face.

"You don't believe what you just saw, do you, Bill?" he chuckled.

"What do you mean?" I asked.

"This is a Hollywood version," he laughed. "They just did this one for the movies."

Sitting there, looking down at the field, I thought maybe he had something there at that.

My main forte up to now with NBC had been football, but in June, I made my biggest single step up the ladder in general sports reporting, when I was picked to handle the blow-by-blow account of the Joe Louis-Tony Galento heavyweight championship fight at Yankee Stadium. The sponsor was the Schick razor blade company and I am convinced that this bout, more than any other, finally awakened Gillette to the importance of sports broadcasting in which they are so prominent today. The day after that bout the Schick people could not keep up with the demand for their product, and razors and blades had to be rushed from the factory to various stores by taxicab. It was a dramatic demonstration of what sports broadcast or, as the case is today, a telecast, can do for a product.

Reviews of my description of the bout, in which Louis came back to knock out Galento after almost being knocked out himself, were excellent, and shortly afterward Sam Taub and I began broadcasting all of the late Mike Jacobs' fistic productions under the sponsorship of Adams Hats.

Now, too, NBC began to move me into other sports. One of the wackiest experiences I had was when Mike Jacobs decided to promote jai alai in the Hippodrome and NBC assigned me to broadcast a portion. Desperately I looked around for someone who knew something about the game and, as he had done before years ago in Paris, Fred Waring came to my rescue. Together we put on one of the strangest broadcasts ever heard. Waring knew the game and all its phases and expressions. But he lost even me. Both jai alai and our broadcasting quickly faded from the Hippodrome.

After football, fight broadcasts had become my main job and I did them with Sam Taub until May, 1941, when, after the Joe Louis-Buddy Baer bout in Washington, NBC lost the shows to Mutual and Gillette. NBC at the time was paying Mike Jacobs $94,000 a year for the bouts, which they in turn sold to Adams Hats. Gillette wanted the sponsorship but wasn't interested in entering a competitive bidding match. So they offered Jacobs $200,000 a year provided he would not reveal the offer until he was ready to sign a formal contract. Jacobs accepted and we at NBC were stunned to lose the bouts.

To be cut out of the fights, I felt, was a great blow to my career. However, now it seems but one of many disappointments as the years slid past. Yet looking back on those early days of my radio career, I realize how fortunate I was.

They were riotous, fantastic years in the growing industry. For instance, Abe Schechter, the hard-hitting former newspaperman who organized NBC's news department, would do almost anything to get the network into print.

Typical of this era was a singing mice contest, which Abe dreamed up.

As far as I have ever been able to discover, mice don't sing. But we collected them from all over the country in a campaign conducted by our local stations.

The stations recorded the mousy "voices" and these records were shipped to New York where we held a judging contest. All we had, in the final analysis, was a quantity of weird sound effects but it must be admitted that the novel press agentry did obtain for us all kinds of free newspaper space.

This was the heyday of radio, which was just then growing out of its swaddling clothes. And I was growing right along with it.

Chapter 7

From the lowly earth
to the vaulted skies.
—Josiah Gilbert Holland

EVEN THOUGH FINANCIALLY Harriet and I were on shaky ground in those first few years, fame and success and their accompanying rewards came with startling swiftness in what were, for me, the furious '40's and the frantic, and finally desperate, '50's.

My career received its first major boost in 1940 when I moved into first place ahead of Ted Husing in the *Radio Daily* poll, which he had dominated for nine straight years. I was to hold that top spot for thirteen consecutive years, by the balloting of the nation's radio editors.

Suddenly I was a "name"; a sought after personality. I picked All-America football teams for *Life* magazine and then for *Look*. I wrote countless magazine articles and was featured in others. I judged beauty contests, made innumerable speaking appearances, and was headlined at sportsmen's shows. There were Bill Stern games and books.

My picture appeared in endorsements for land developments, clothing, candies, motorcycles, sunglasses, butter, summer resorts, cigarettes, hats, typewriters, and even barber shops. I recorded albums featuring dramatic stories of sports events, and I bought a cabin cruiser which Dinah Shore and Lina Romay helped me christen.

Harriet and I moved into a plush, terraced apartment on East 79th Street in Manhattan where we lived when Peter was born in May, 1940, and until after Mary arrived in January, 1944, and Patty in March, 1950. But I didn't see enough of it or them, unfortunately.

I was here, there, and everywhere, broadcasting all of the major sports events, from the Rose Bowl to the Olympic games in England. In addition to *Radio Daily,* awards came in clusters from such valued sources as *Motion Picture Daily, Radio and Television Mirror,* Scripps-Howard and other newspapers. Most of this acclaim was due to my Friday night Colgate show which, running from October of 1939 through 1951, was always lucrative but at one period brought me as much as $2,500 a week.

Soon, too, Hollywood summoned me. Through a span of fifteen perpetual motion years I did two M-G-M newsreels a week. I turned out one filmed sport short a month for Columbia pictures and appeared in a half-dozen motion pictures, including *Pride of the Yankees,* the story of Lou Gehrig of the New York Yankees; *We've Never Been Licked,* a film about Texas A. & M.; *Stage Door Canteen;* an Abbott and Costello tickler titled *Here Come The Co-eds;* and *The West Point Story.*

It was the kind of success which, I am quite certain, would have gone to almost anybody's head. But it remained for

Samuel Goldwyn, the motion picture genius, to take some of the wind out of my sails when I first went to Hollywood—at long last an actor such as I had dreamed of in those early days after my graduation from P.M.C. and that first abortive trip to the motion picture capitol—to appear in *Pride of the Yankees*.

On arrival at the lot I was told that Mr. Goldwyn wanted to see me. Undoubtedly, I thought, he is interested in meeting Bill Stern. Quite impressed with myself I walked condescendingly into his inner sanctum and then stood there with growing discomfort as he continued going through some papers in front of him. Finally he looked up and asked me abruptly, "What do you do?"

Somewhat taken aback, I replied, "I'm Bill Stern. I'm a sports announcer."

"Are you any good?"

"Well," I hedged, "I hope so."

"They tell me you're pretty good," he nodded. "I guess you'll do." Then he waved me away.

Gary Cooper and Teresa Wright were the stars of the picture, in which I had what was actually a bit part. The picture ran into several delays and one weekend it was necessary to shoot a sequence in which I was involved, on a Sunday. It was raining, everyone was in bad humor at having to work overtime, and the director was screaming that every second's delay was costing thousands of dollars.

Just after one of these harangues a studio guard came onto the set and told the director he would have to hold up shooting. "Mr. Goldwyn wants Mr. Stern on the telephone," he said.

The closest phone was two blocks away on an outside telephone pole. Following the guard, I sloshed through the rain to take the call, the water ruining my makeup and running off the end of my nose in a varicolored cascade. All I could see was thousands of dollars going up in smoke.

"This is Bill Stern," I said.

"Goldwyn here. Say Stern, was your mother Lena Reis from Cincinnati?"

"Yes," I replied, "she was."

"Well, what do you know about that," Goldwyn said. "I think I was at her wedding in Cincinnati." There was a pause and then he added, "Well, I just wondered. Give her my regards."

Then he hung up and I splashed, mystified at the wonderful workings of Hollywood, back to the set where everybody was waiting. The shooting went on as if nothing had happened. After all, nobody, not even the director, was going to complain about Sam Goldwyn's interruption no matter how many dollars it cost.

In the early part of this period of my life I also was privileged to take part in two television firsts. One was the first remote control sports broadcast ever attempted and the second was the first telecast of a professional baseball game, both strictly experimental.

The first experiment was conducted in May, 1939, when NBC sent me to Columbia University's baseball field, on the tip of Manhattan and adjacent to Baker Field, to telecast the Columbia-Princeton game. This was the initial baseball game to be televised, and in an era when there were very few home sets the engineers wished to see what would happen when the cameras were moved outdoors. This test proved that baseball telecasts were feasible.

All through the war years there was little experimentation in television for entertainment purposes, but NBC remained busy in its laboratories. Thus, early in the war cameras were set up in the Polo Grounds and I did a New York Giants-St.

Louis Cardinals game, so that engineers and technicians could work out some of the bugs. I remember thinking that someday there would be many games televised. And we learned, even with that first professional baseball telecast, that more than one camera would be needed and that their proper location would be highly important.

My greatest rivalry throughout these days was with Ted Husing, the ace sports announcer for the Columbia Broadcasting System and a man with a crisp, authoritative voice. It is only natural, I suppose, that he should have resented me, particularly after I regularly began to displace him at the top of various polls.

We were thrown together a great deal, because as I took over the major sports events for NBC Ted was covering them for CBS. He left no doubt that he considered me an imitator, although I honestly didn't feel that I was. After one Notre Dame football game, while we were both standing in the South Bend station waiting for the train to take us back to New York, I admired a sports jacket he was wearing.

"That's a beautiful jacket," I told him, asking idly, "where did you get it, Ted?"

Husing, always impeccable and capable of adopting a scathing tone, drew himself up haughtily, gave me a scornful look, and said sarcastically, "My God, Stern, now are you going to start copying my clothes, too?"

Each of us did everything we could to plague the other. There was one occasion when I almost ruined myself trying to pull a fast one on him.

We were both at an Illinois-Army game in Champaign, Illinois, and the NBC and CBS booths were side-by-side on the top of the triple-deck stadium. Our cable lines ran along a narrow concrete ledge in front of the booths, and on a moment's impulse I slipped a pair of cutting pliers from our engineer's bag, edged my way precariously out on the narrow ledge, and proceeded to snip what I thought were Husing's lines. It never entered my head that one slip of my foot would plunge me to my death. Crawling back inside of my own booth, I sat there with satanic delight waiting for my cue to take the air at 1:45 P.M., fifteen minutes before game time.

But I was filled with consternation as, at the appointed moment, there was no cue for us to start on NBC. Through the thin panel separating us from Husing I dimly could hear Ted opening right on the dot for CBS. Frantically my engineer scrambled out on the ledge and returned shortly with a disgusted look on his face.

"You're a real genius," he growled.

"What was the matter?" I demanded.

"You," he replied with scorn, "cut our lines by mistake."

Both of us were in difficulty on another occasion when we broadcast the Vanderbilt-Alabama football game from Nashville. Our booths, as usual, were perched high atop the rim of the stadium, and when we arrived we discovered that early that same morning some wag had freshly painted both booths, inside and out, with gray paint, which by the end of the afternoon had all of us daubed like Indians. But the perpetrator hadn't let it go at that. On the door to Husing's booth there was painted, in large letters, a sign which said "Ladies." On the door to my booth had been painted "Men." We spent the entire afternoon trying to stay out of fresh paint and directing urgent and persistent ladies and gentlemen in other directions.

Another time NBC had bought exclusive rights to the U.S. Amateur Athletic Association's annual national track and field championships. These were to be broadcast from the Marquette University stadium in Milwaukee, and when I began checking over the arrangements everything was fine except for one item.

Overlooking the stadium was a towering church spire and on top of it a platform had been erected, complete right down to a huge beach umbrella. It was obvious to me that Husing intended to bootleg the track meet from outside the stadium with the use of high-powered binoculars as well as by monitoring my broadcast. My suspicions were confirmed shortly when Husing appeared on the platform.

Irritated, I sought out the pastor of the church and explained that NBC had bought exclusive rights to the meet. The minister, a mild, smiling man, replied gently that there was nothing he could do.

"We couldn't possibly ask Mr. Husing to get off the steeple," he said. "Mr. Husing is a God-fearing man and besides he made a substantial cash contribution to the church."

Hastening to the telephone company I ordered them to install two poles directly in line of Husing's vision. Between these we strung huge sheets of cheesecloth. That Husing was ingenious. He simply bought some firecrackers and threw them into the cheesecloth. It vanished in a puff of smoke.

Refusing to be beaten I searched around and hired two mammoth klieg lights to shine up into his eyes. But they were no sooner set up than they had to be discarded on orders of our legal department, which ruled that Husing could sue us on grounds of having done permanent damage to his eyes. We knew, however, that he couldn't see enough of the meet to do it properly without monitoring my broadcast. New York instructed me to make a few intentional mistakes, such as having certain runners fall down when they hadn't. By monitoring his broadcast, NBC found that, within moments, Husing had the same runner falling.

Throughout the rest of the afternoon I made just enough intentional mistakes to hang him. NBC officials summoned CBS officials the following Monday and played back recordings of both broadcasts to show that he had imitated everything I had done, proved, of course, by the intentional mistakes.

As a result of this incident, the networks got together and decided there would be no more piracy. But it didn't last long. Competition was keen and soon we both were back at it.

I did my share, too. Shortly thereafter it was CBS which came up with an exclusive, this time on the Poughkeepsie Regatta. Our legal department decided, cautiously, that while Husing had exclusive rights to broadcast from the observation train which followed the race along the riverbank, nobody had a legal option on the Hudson River.

Thereupon NBC put me atop a house overlooking the Hudson at Poughkeepsie, from which I had a fine view of the water but little else. The four-mile course was impossible to see so I simply listened to Husing broadcast from the observation train, dressed up his report, and repeated his information.

There was just one difficulty.

The usually accurate Husing called the wrong winner.

So did Bill Stern.

Husing's mistake naturally became mine, too. But it wasn't my first, or my last. I have, over the years, taken a great deal of ribbing for my facility in coming out of these situations right side up. Sometimes you just don't have time to make corrections—such as the occasion when I had Doc Blanchard of Army running "all by himself" for a touchdown, "down to the thirty, the twenty, the ten. . . ."

Then, to my consternation, I saw that it was Glenn Davis.

Without dropping a syllable I snapped, "And he laterals off to Glenn Davis, who goes over for the touchdown."

Sure, it was a boner and, certainly, I covered it up quickly. Was anybody really hurt in the process? I don't believe so. The vast radio audience had enjoyed a smooth description of a football game. Had I called attention to my error, many listeners might have felt I was balling up the whole game with corrections or would have begun wondering how many other mistakes I was making.

Sometime later, when I went to the Kentucky Derby, I asked Clem McCarthy how he thought I might do with a horse race.

"Okay," Clem said, "but remember, you can't lateral a horse."

I was, for a while, quite sensitive about this needling which, on occasion, certainly had a basis in fact. Yet I honestly feel, even in a newly discovered ability to face facts and call a spade a spade, that much of the time the criticism was overdone.

Extraordinary financial success and the renown which radio brought to me carried with them, as I should have expected, an unavoidable amount of jealousy, criticism, and character assassination which I suppose, in looking back over the years, I should have accepted complacently as an occupational hazard.

Whatever the price, it is worth it if your only gauge is success. And success I had in heaping measure, capped in May, 1951, by the winning of the National Academy of Television Arts and Sciences Emmy award, which is to radio what the Oscar is to Hollywood. The Emmy awards are especially coveted because they are voted on by members of the profession.

The night they were announced, in the grand ballroom of

the Waldorf-Astoria before 1,200 leaders of the industry, I had already been awarded honors of the year in sports broadcasting by *Radio Daily, Motion Picture Daily, Radio and Television Mirror,* and *Liberty* magazine. This one, the most prized of all, would give me a clean sweep.

When my name was announced as the winner a great lump leaped into my throat and tears came to my eyes. The walk forward seemed like a dream and yet it was the shortest and easiest I had ever made on my artificial leg. There was a flight of steps to the stage but no steps before, or since, have been so easy to negotiate. I skipped up them.

It was the proudest moment of my life.

Chapter 8

The most wasted day of all is that on which we have not laughed.

—Sébastien Chamfort

THERE WAS A GRIM SIDE to these years, days and nights of utter desperation which still shake me as I recall them. It is only now, with newfound clarity, that I can appreciate the lighter side of some of my experiences, as well as the humor, which once bounced off the outer shell of Bill Stern like hail from a taut umbrella.

Time, it is said, heals all wounds. And yet I wonder even now whether Graham McNamee or the state of Iowa ever recovered from an incident which happened early in my radio career and still tickles my funny bone?

We were doing an Iowa-Notre Dame football game, an event which Iowans rank in the same category as a presidential election. Graham, a man who abhorred anything west of

Broadway, was of the privately hoarded opinion that Marquette and Joliet, as well as Lewis and Clark, would have done better to make wide detours around the state of Iowa and leave it to the Indians in undiscovered anonymity.

As we finished the broadcast Graham gave his standard closing, "This is Graham McNamee, speaking from Iowa, and saying good night. . . ."

Glancing simultaneously at the engineer, he received the cue that the circuit had been cut and, almost in the same breath, McNamee added soulfully, " . . . thank God!"

The circuit, unfortunately, hadn't been cut. The entire state of Iowa descended by telephone, telegraph, and letter on the discomfited Graham.

I had my moments of anguish, too, such as the afternoon in Tyler, Texas, when I stood at the siding waiting with microphone in hand for the approach of the Baylor football team. We were going to give it the full treatment with a color description of the arrival of their special train—the coaches, the team, the band, and the excitement.

Suddenly around a curve in the track steamed a locomotive and excitedly I snapped into the cue line back to the local station, "Give me the air."

Immediately I got it and began to broadcast my description—as a 103-car freight train jolted past with a cargo of hogs, cows, chickens, and vegetables. So I described what I saw—the hogs, cows, chickens, and vegetables.

Still green in memory, too, are the sideline incidents when Harold Vanderbilt's *Ranger* creamed T. O. M. Sopwith's *Endeavor II* in four straight races during the America's Cup races at Newport in 1937. This was the event from which we had been relieved by Abe Schechter for injudicious use of our communications wave length.

Setting a personal tempo for the races, the late Jack Miley

of the New York *Daily News* rapped at the door of my hotel room the first night. He was quite casual as I opened up and greeted him.

"Bill, would you like to see the damnedest fire you ever saw?" he asked me with a quizzical grin.

"I sure would," I told him.

"Well," he said casually, "come on down to my room."

Unhurriedly he led me down the hall to his room and then, in the manner of a theatrical impresario, flung open the door.

He was right. Inside, blazing merrily, was, as he had said, one of the damnedest fires I've ever seen. I reached for the telephone to call the desk.

Sopwith, the multimillionaire airplane builder from England who was challenging for the America's Cup, was hot news in Great Britain. Arrangements had been made with NBC to feed the British Broadcasting Corporation.

After two races, in which Sopwith's *Endeavor II* had been clobbered by the American boat, I did a special program for the BBC in which I interviewed experts attending the races. One of these was sharp-witted Henry McLemore, who was covering the event for the United Press.

"Have you heard," he asked innocently on the air, "that Sopwith is requesting a one day's postponement?"

I hadn't, and sensing important news asked, "Why?"

"So," said Henry with exaggerated deliberation, "he can go to a psychiatrist and have his head examined for even showing up."

This made such a great hit in Great Britain that we had to apologize to the BBC. Despite this experience I invited Henry back onto the show after the third race in which Sopwith, *Endeavor II,* and Great Britain had taken another beating.

McLemore was terse and straight to the point. "I understand," he intoned, "that the United States tonight is presenting Mr. Sopwith a paid-up social security card. After one more defeat he can retire right here in the United States and won't have to go back to England at all."

Track and field always has been a great favorite of mine and I was fortunate to get to know such great gentlemen as Glenn Cunningham and another miler named Archie San Romani. One afternoon there was a meet at Princeton which I was broadcasting, and Archie approached me rather hesitantly.

"Bill," he said, "at almost any moment my wife is going to have a baby out in Kansas. The hospital didn't know where to contact me immediately so I told them to get in touch with NBC and to telephone you if anything happens."

"Archie," I replied, "I'll be glad to let you know as soon as I hear anything."

The race was just about to start when the news came that the baby had been born and both mother and child were doing fine. Standing up and waving my arms wildly, I managed to attract Archie's eyes and I clasped my hands over my head, like a prize fighter being introduced, in congratulations. Then they were off.

Archie didn't win, but he ran farther than the rest of them. For, as he crossed the finish line, he kept right on going, through the ramp, up the steps of Palmer Stadium and all the way to the NBC booth. He was breathless when he burst in and grabbed my hand.

"What am I, Bill," he gasped, "a mother or a father?"

There was another occasion on which I was to broadcast an important tennis match when Don Budge and Gene Mako were teamed up at Newport to defend their national doubles championship. The match was scheduled for eleven o'clock in the morning, and promptly at the appointed time I took the air.

There was just one difficulty. The minutes dragged on . . . 11:10 . . . 11:15 . . . 11:30 . . . and no Budge or Mako. I had described everything I could think of, the weather, the tournament, the Casino, the people in attendance, various players, and was working desperately through the rules and history of tennis when finally, at 11:40, they strolled out on the court.

After the match ended and I had wearily signed off, I sought out Budge and asked him with some irritation what had caused the delay in their appearance.

"Why," Don said with surprise, "didn't you know that Tommy Dorsey's band was on the air this morning? I'm a great Dorsey fan, so Gene and I just had to wait until he went off the air."

So, while he and Mako sat enjoying Tommy Dorsey's music over rival CBS, I was sweating it out with an open mike killing time on NBC.

The annual birthday ball for the late President Roosevelt always was a gala affair, to which were invited many stars of stage, screen, and radio. One of the yearly traditions was a huge birthday cake which Mrs. Roosevelt cut while the newsreel cameras ground away. But during one of the war years, when sugar rationing was at its height, it was decided that there should be a fake cake made out of wood and merely iced over.

Nobody remembered, however, to tell Mrs. Roosevelt.

As the time came for the cake cutting ceremony we all gathered around her in the White House and Mrs. Roosevelt waited with poised knife for the signal from the newsreel corps. When it came, she brought down the knife and there was a resounding thud. The knife almost was knocked from her hand. Mrs. Roosevelt was quite flustered but Betty Grable saved the day. Looking at Carol Bruce, Betty quipped brightly, "I knew I left that damned cake in the oven too long!"

We all howled, and yet it was no laughing matter at another birthday ball a couple of years later when Jo Stafford, Eileen Barton, and I were braced by a Secret Service agent just after we had "appropriated" souvenirs of our White House visit.

The girls had slipped tiny demitasse saucers into their purses and I had pocketed a silver spoon bearing the presidential crest, while we were sitting alone at a small table. Hardly had they disappeared from sight when the agent casually seated himself with us.

"You know," he began very conversationally, "every single piece of furniture, silver, and china, right down to the ash trays, is checked and inventoried after we have guests here in the White House."

"I suppose you have to do that, with all the souvenir seekers who come here," Jo replied in sweet innocence.

"That's right," he acknowledged. "You'd be surprised at some of the people who would stoop to this kind of petty larceny. But, believe me, as soon as anything is missing, we know it."

The tiny spoon by now was burning a guilty hole in my pocket and did so throughout the next half-hour as we were taken on a tour of the White House. That fragment of silver, which hangs over my desk now, was paid for in full in appresensive perspiration by the time we left. I'm certain the agent knew all about our little souvenirs, but he didn't embarrass us with a formal request that they be returned.

Another who loved to put me on a "spot" was Leo Durocher, in the days when he managed the erstwhile

Brooklyn Dodgers. There was one period in which, wherever I went, hordes of bright young men would turn up at the various studios seeking auditions from me.

"Leo Durocher said to tell you he sent me," was the invariable comment.

Finally I decided to get even. That winter, wherever I went, I sought out young ballplayers and told them that off the record I was scouting baseball talent for the Dodgers. My advice to them was to see Durocher either during spring training or whenever the Dodgers were in Brooklyn or in their town.

"Tell Leo that I sent you," I advised them.

Durocher was inundated by my "prospects" all spring and into the summer. Eventually I received a supplicating wire from him.

PLEASE CALL OFF YOUR GYPSIES. I GIVE UP.

I almost gave up myself while broadcasting the Masters golf tournament from Augusta, Georgia, in 1948. It was a beautiful day and I was cruising around the course in a jeep, describing everything of interest, when I noticed a tremendous crowd banked about a distant green. Driving closer, I was able to see that they were watching that perennial favorite, Sam Snead.

As I neared the green the crowd scattered to head for the next tee, and I intercepted Sam as he walked past me with his caddy. Leaning down, I held the mike in front of him and asked, "How are you, Sam?"

What I didn't know was that Snead had just blown a two-foot putt, a soul-searing performance for a professional golfer.

So Sam thundered an instant reply. "I," he said, "am a son of a bitch."

My engineer's alertness saved the situation. He had observed the storm clouds on Sam's brow and when he heard Snead start the "son of a . . ." he clipped it off and the last word never got on the air.

There is nothing humorous about baldness and at an earlier age, certainly, than I expected, I began to be afflicted with what is referred to as a receding hairline. This is to most men a distinct blow to their vanity. When you appear on television it is, in some cases, sheer tragedy. Thus, at one point in my career I decided that it behooved me to get a hairpiece to camouflage my advancing cranial nakedness.

Shortly after this, I left my home in Purchase, already late, to drive to New York for a television appearance. I was well on my way when I realized, to my consternation, that I had left my new hairpiece at home. There was nothing to do but turn around and go back for it. By the time I did, and started again for New York, I was far behind schedule and was driving faster than the law allows. Within a few miles there was the wail of a siren and a motorcycle policeman motioned me over to the side of the road.

"What's the hurry?" he asked.

I was anxious to get moving again. "Officer," I said, "if I can give you a new excuse that you haven't heard before will you skip the ticket and let me be on my way?"

He grinned hugely. "Brother, you couldn't give me a new one. I've heard them all."

"It's this way," I explained after he laughingly told me to give it a try, "the reason I'm speeding is that I had to go back home for my hairpiece and now I'm late for a television broadcast."

With that I took the lid off the box, which was on the seat beside me, and waved the hairpiece in his face.

"I thought I'd heard everything," he admitted. "Okay, you win. Get going."

I wasn't so fortunate another time when I was late for an engagement in Boston. As I whipped through a small town in Connecticut near the Massachusetts line a motorcycle policeman again pulled me over for speeding, but this fellow didn't waste any time. Without delay he ordered me to follow him to the local magistrate.

"Look," I told the magistrate, "I'm Bill Stern, the radio sports commentator, and . . ."

That's as far as I got. The magistrate held up a restraining hand and interrupted:

"Look yourself, son. We had Franklin D. Roosevelt, Jr. in here the other day and *he* paid his twenty-five dollars."

So did I.

Chapter 9

Defamed by every charlatan,
And soiled with all ignoble use.
—Alfred, Lord Tennyson

UNKNOWN TO ANYONE, except possibly Harriet, there was a dreary, dismal undercurrent to what on the surface appeared to be a glamorous, swift moving, and highly successful career. Immediately after my release from the hospital in 1935 I fought an up and down battle, losing ground constantly in my attempts to get off sleeping pills.

I had never been what you might call a good sleeper and not even the periods of sheer exhaustion from the hectic pace at which I was living ever really precluded the necessity of their use. Inadvertently in more relaxed moments, scant as they were, I reached for the sleeping pill bottle after tossing and turning for hours without approaching slumber.

This created a circle of catastrophe. Sleep-drugged mornings were counteracted with pep pills in a constant clash between barbiturate and Benzedrine.

The three years after my leg amputation were an endless struggle to readjust myself and attempt to learn to live with pain.

Although my stump did not ache constantly it tormented me intermittently. A change in the weather brought on an unrelenting, hammering ache. The nerve ends quivered spasmodically of their own volition at periodic intervals. There also were what are known as phantom pains: the feeling that you still had the missing leg and that, somehow, it was hurting.

Then there were other complications, physical and mental. In 1939, while the leg was still an unending source of pain and irritation, I began to have frequent kidney stone attacks. These, at least from my experience, are among the most agonizing ailments a man could possibly have. In those days there were no truly effective dissolvents and a series of doctors met each crisis, in which I was convulsed with severe stomach, back, and leg pains, by giving me injections of morphine. These injections not only eased the pain but also relaxed the nervous system, so that the stone could be passed.

All of this agony was compounded by a feeling through the years, whenever I had an event snatched away from me, that the old prejudices were at work; by insecurity and an emotional instability of which, at that time, I was in total ignorance; by an unrelenting ambition which had its tentacles in my childhood; and by the strain under which I worked feverishly and without letup.

In addition to this physical and mental anguish, I was in a business which kept me on edge. In radio and television there is the constant fear that you will say something wrong over the air. Preparing new shows, and always trying to im-

Bill Stern, 1941, NBC's first Sports Director

Left: "One-yard Kelly" at P.M.C., 1928

Above: Bill, his mother, and his elder brother Tom

Below: At P.M.C. in his freshman year

Above left: Bill Stern, Dinah Shore, Lena Romay, and Budd Hulick aboard *Wee Pete*

Above center: Broadcasting one of his many football games

Above right: Telecasting a game, 1954

Below: A studio interview: Chuck Dressen, former manager of the Brooklyn Dodgers, Bill, and Fred Haney, manager of the Milwaukee Braves, during the 1954 World Series

Right: Bill helps Edgar Bergen give Charlie McCarthy a pep talk before he leaves the bench

Below: An early broadcast with Walter Winchell

Above: Interviewing Eleanor Roosevelt on his successful Sports Newsreel show

Below left: On the air with Eleanor Powell, one of his early girl friends

Below right: Maureen O'Sullivan reads the comics to Bill

Harriet and Bill at a fishing camp in Canada, 1952

Relaxing beside his pool at his home in Purchase, New York

Broadcasting from his poolside cabaña

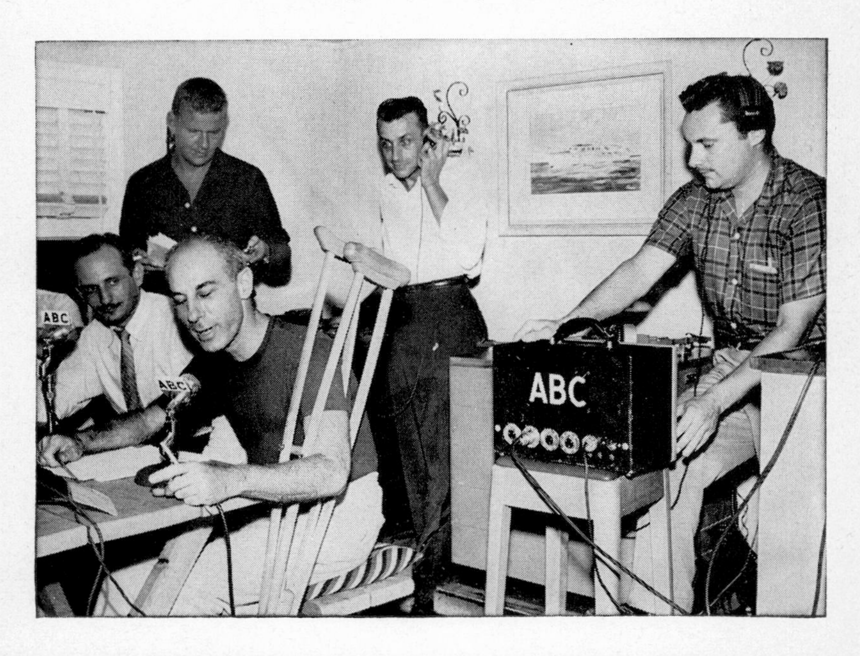

Broadcasting a television first, 1939

prove on them so as to stay at the top of the ever-shifting heap, made me just that much more of a slave to my emotions.

The turmoil inside me was complicated, too, by several more narrow escapes from death.

In 1939, at about the time when the kidney stone attacks were commencing, I went to Lincoln, Nebraska, to broadcast the National Amateur Athletic Union's annual track and field championships. To facilitate this coverage I had devised a portable broadcasting stand which revolved on casters. The stand rotated in such a manner that I could watch the runners all the way around the oval track without twisting myself into a pretzel.

During this meet at the Nebraska Memorial Stadium there was a violent rain and thunder storm. The meet was halted and I had walked barely a hundred feet from my stand when it was struck by a blinding bolt of lightning. The bewildering crash stunned me but it completely demolished the stand, splintering it into a heap of scorched fragments.

All I could do was stand there in the rain, staring at the wrecked stand and quivering with the realization of my narrow escape.

There was another, and far worse, brush with death the following year and this one, too, had to do with a track meet. It was a placid spring evening when I boarded the New York Central's Commodore Vanderbilt for an overnight trip to Chicago, where I was to air a track meet and also put Dizzy Dean on the radio during my stay there.

After reading for a while in my bedroom I rang for the porter and had him make up my berth. Then, just before eleven o'clock that night, as the train approached Little Falls, New York, I undressed, took off my artificial leg and put on my pajamas. I had hardly crawled into my berth and snapped off the light when all hell broke loose.

The train lurched drunkenly. There was a sickening series of horrifying noises, the train bumping, grinding, and ripping, and I was tossed in all directions in the darkness. I wound up in a heap in a corner of my berth as the train finally toppled over on its side. Glass shattered and I seemed to be riding a bucking demon interminably through an ebony pit while shrieks of pain and terror slashed through the nightmare from all sides of me. The hammering motion ended at last and for a few shocked moments there was an awful stillness. Then screams tore through the darkness in a rising crescendo.

Fumbling around in the darkness I managed somehow to locate my artificial leg. Ripping off my pajamas I strapped it on, and groping through the welter around me felt out my clothing. It seemed an eternity before I could get dressed. From above me, where a window had been shattered, I could smell fresh air. Incoherently I prayed there would be no fire as I clambered awkwardly into my clothes and then somehow clawed my way out through the window and scrambled to the ground. Others were emerging, too, shouting frantically for their loved ones, moaning or screaming in pain and terror, or merely standing wordlessly in shock.

The train had gone into a curve too rapidly and had jumped the track. The other end of the car in which I was riding had been telescoped by the car behind it. Thirty-two persons had been killed in the crash, twelve of them in my car where the opposite end had been crushed completely.

Panting from my exertions, and as shaken as I was, I looked wildly for someplace where I might find a telephone. NBC should have news of this. Crunching across the roadbed and making my way through a field, I headed for the lights of a gasoline station which I could see on a parallel highway and the telephone which I figured would be there. Someone asked me if I was hurt and then provided me with change, and I telephoned NBC.

Within ten minutes after I had crawled from the wreckage I was put through to Abe Schechter, who was in charge of news and special events. Swiftly, if somewhat incoherently, I explained what had happened. Abe reacted like a veteran.

"Hold that line open," he barked, remembering only then to ask me whether I was all right. "We'll put you right on the air from the scene of the accident and you can do a spot description."

A few minutes later he was back and now his voice was low and I could feel that he was fighting to control it. "Sorry, Bill," he said bitterly. "We can't do it."

I was utterly amazed. "What do you mean, we can't do it?" I stuttered.

"I'm sorry, we just can't use it. I'll fill you in on it when you get back to New York from Chicago."

Schechter said that he would let Harriet know immediately that I was all right and, happily, she didn't even know about the accident until they called her.

Several days later, when I returned to New York, Abe told me what had happened to keep NBC from a tremendous news "beat."

He had telephoned John Royal while I waited on the open line at Little Falls but, unfortunately, financial aspects have a way occasionally of interfering with facts; as I know all too well.

Royal, inspecting the over-all picture, realized that New York Central was a major account with the Lord and Thomas advertising agency which, in turn, directed much lucrative business to NBC. He theorized that our eye-witness broadcast might alienate Lord and Thomas, so we were cancelled out before we ever got on the air.

At about this time my kidney stone attacks had reached a nerve-shattering peak which I could hardly bear, and the physician who was attending me recommended that I see a urology specialist and I followed his advice.

As events developed, he was to be my personal Machiavelli.

He will always live in my memory as a devil, and I find it almost impossible to believe that there could be men such as he among the dedicated disciples of Hippocrates. For slowly and with insidious surety he made me, with conscious design, ever more dependent on him for the relieving solace of the morphine needle and, it might be added, at staggering prices.

From the very first he injected me on the slightest provocation and at the first hint of pain, and I did pass several stones. The morphine build-up was insidiously gradual and, when there was no disappearance of the kidney pains, after about six months he ordered me into a New York hospital for a complete examination.

After it was made, I was completely unnerved when he told me that he had discovered a papilloma, a type of malignant tumor, and only his injections calmed me as I underwent a cystotomy to have it removed.

After the cystotomy, when he visited me, I asked him, "That was cancerous, wasn't it?"

"How did you know?" he inquired, answering my question with another. Then he informed me that he had removed several tumors from inside my kidney.

"We will have to keep a very close and continual check on you to make certain that they don't recur," he said.

The usual procedure in undergoing my almost weekly cystoscopy, in which a tube is passed through the urinary track so that the bladder walls can be inspected, was for me to check into the hospital the preceding night. I was allowed no breakfast, but after being given an injection of morphine or Demerol I was taken to the operating room and the cystoscopy was performed.

It was such a nerve-raking and painful ordeal that I would do almost anything to stay under sedation. Eventually I always claimed pain so that the soothing injection would be forthcoming.

Also, it must be admitted, I was beginning to like the effect of the drug.

Meanwhile, there was no limit placed by the doctor on the amount of drugs which I was permitted, and I soon discovered that every time I rang for the nurse more drugs would be administered. It was such obvious overdosing that several nurses at the hospital warned me that they thought surely I was being given too much morphine, yet there was nothing they could do about it as it was being given under the doctor's orders.

Strangely enough, at this time the craving had not had the slightest derogatory effect on my work. And, except for this growing need, life was good to Harriet and me. While she knew of the drugs from the beginning, Harriet did not believe that I was in any sense becoming addicted and thought as long as it did not affect my work or my voice that I could control any urge in that direction. I thought so, too. We had a beautiful terraced apartment in Manhattan, I was earning big money, and we were overjoyed when our son, Peter, was born in May, 1940.

Yet, by the end of 1941, after long months of constant checkups on my kidney condition, the drugs had an iron grip on me and I was conscious of the fact that I was thinking of having injections even when I wasn't going to the hospital.

By now I was visiting this doctor every weekend for a shot, and with this gradual build-up at the end of two years I also started receiving an injection during the middle of the week. This, despite the fact that by this time my hospital checkups had been reduced to once a month. Then, as the build-up progressed, in succeeding months he would give me an injection at any hour of the day or night if I claimed that I was in pain.

I remember at about this time listening to a drama on the radio about drug addiction which made me stop momentarily and wonder whether it had any bearing on my case. But I shrugged it off as an utter impossibility.

At about this time, however, I did make my first conscientious effort to bring it to a halt. I decided that I would not call him for additional appointments and would take an injection only when I went to the hospital for a cystoscopy. This I managed to do for several months, and since I could satisfy myself that I was only taking morphine at the hospital because of the pain involved in undergoing the cystoscopy, I was able to deceive myself that I was not in any shape or manner becoming an addict.

I was living in a fool's paradise.

After another year I could no longer restrict my need for drugs merely to my monthly hospital visits and I found more and more excuses to visit the doctor.

Never once did he show the slightest reluctance to taking care of my "pain." There was just one occasion in those early days, while he prepared the syringe and waved it in front of my hungry eyes, that he observed in passing, "You know, Bill, this isn't good for you."

I realize that this is a terrible charge that I make. Yet I

am absolutely positive that he knew what he was doing to me.

I say this with a full knowledge of the accusation I am making. It wasn't until long after I was well "hooked" that he patronizingly preached to me about the evil effects of what we were doing; preached while holding the morphine syringe ready in front of me and watching almost sadistically my dry-lipped longing for the injection.

I listened, nodded, and held out my arm.

And the needle was always there.

I do not, however, place the complete blame on him. He could not have done this to a person who was physically well and who was not susceptible to the proddings of a horde of inner demons. Still, he should have known, far better than I, what the effect of this dreadful thing would be. His reason, and I say this accusingly, was, I am positive, as much for the sadistic pleasure he obtained from seeing me in this condition as it was for the tremendous sums of money I was paying him.

By 1945 I had become so accustomed to drugs—morphine, Demerol, and Dilaudid—that I *had* to have them. I realized now the terrible effects and constantly attempted to cut down, waging this battle through the next five years without any great success; wanting them badly, trying to rationalize, but realizing that for my own well-being I must stop.

Never did I inoculate myself; some small if rather inconceivable consolation.

But I had found that by faking stomach cramps or a kidney stone attack or leg pains, doctors almost anywhere would give me an injection.

Many times in my travels I would arrive in a hotel in a strange city and summon the house doctor. Ordinarily he would not be suspicious of a so-called celebrity coming through town like this and would gladly consent to give me what I wanted.

Whether in those early years immediately after the accident I was enslaved to the degree that I had to have drugs I do not know; I know I wanted them. Whether if I had tried determinedly to shake loose at this stage I could have done so I don't know either.

I do know that I didn't try as I should have.

I enjoyed the effects: the peace and calm induced within me; the knowledge that I was a wonderfully accomplished person, superior to others; the confidence that there was no problem I could not conquer; and, of course, the separation from pain. These were feelings I didn't have without drugs and I ignored the fatal toll of not being able to eat, or to live a normal life.

Sleep, even with an ever-growing number of sleeping pills, was a nebulous thing. I dozed fitfully, lying in that land halfway between sleep and wakefulness for hours, hardly conscious when I lit a cigarette. Innumerable times I blistered my fingers and as I dozed more deeply the cigarette would fall unheeded from my hand. I burned ugly holes in sheets, mattresses, blankets, and rugs from one end of the country to the other.

Throughout most of this time I kept telling myself that I could control this urge, but after innumerable voluntary attempts to stop ended in nothingness, by 1950 I was beginning to get desperate.

It was then that I decided on a controlled attempt to take the cure and voluntarily entered a hospital.

I was admitted on a Friday night, and as the first step I was knocked out with Pentothal Sodium. After this, massive amounts of tranquilizers were administered.

They helped only microscopically. I had nightmares, horrible dreams in which once again I was undergoing the removal of my leg. I awakened, over and over again, in a cold sweat which drenched my body from head to toe. Frantically I rang for the nurse and more tranquilizers were administered.

After four days I left the hospital, weak, worn, and exhausted. I had accomplished absolutely nothing and I knew it with dread certainty.

Now, I realized with horrifying sureness, I was a "legal addict."

Chapter 10

Everything that deceives
may be said to enchant.
—Plato

DESPITE THE HIDDEN DESPERATION of those years and my continual backsliding in the matter of drugs, I managed to become fabulously successful financially. The cornerstone of these lucrative times was the Colgate Sports Newsreel show, which I started late in 1939.

In September of that year I was approached by Stuart Sherman. He now is vice-president in charge of Colgate's marketing department, but in those days was with the Benton and Bowles advertising agency in Chicago.

Sherman made me a proposition which, I could see immediately, had unlimited possibilities.

"Your voice is fine and I think maybe Colgate might use you in a radio show if we can work it out in the right format," he told me. "But make no mistake, Bill, it will have to be a sure-fire formula."

The more we talked the more I realized that this was my golden opportunity. He was talking about Colgate as a sponsor and Colgate, then as now, was one of the blue chip advertisers in my business. There was an added factor. Colgate had pulled its business out of NBC a year earlier after a dispute with the network and if I could woo them back it meant that not only would I wind up with one of the nation's top sponsors but also I would be putting a feather in my cap at NBC.

Stuart and I both agreed that a sports show, pure and simple, would do little but chase women listeners away from the radio. The history of the sports show in radio was studded with repeated failures. Searching diligently through the files at NBC, I found that more sports shows had crashed on the rocks of disaster than any other type of program. No sports show of any kind ever had lasted more than one year on a regular basis.

Ted Husing, my talented rival on CBS, had attempted several different types of shows for various sponsors. There had been sports programs devoted exclusively to sports news and anecdotes about sports figures, as well as shows featuring the brightest sports figures of the day: Walter Hagen, Gene Sarazen, Bobby Jones, Jack Dempsey, and others. All of them had faded into costly oblivion.

The list of failures was long and varied. A program featuring Babe Ruth on how to play baseball and one on which Grantland Rice, the dean of sportswriters, used the most famous sports personalities as guests had fallen by the wayside. Rice had done well with a once-a-week show in which he introduced storied football stars, but his had been a Friday night show in which the main lure consisted of predictions on the outcome of the following day's college football games. This show ran only through the football season and left the air during the other nine months. But the records showed clearly that any plain week-in and week-out sports show never had survived beyond one year.

Every big name sports announcer had given it a try, including such talented men as Husing, Graham McNamee, Don Wilson, Bill Slater, and Clem McCarthy. All of them, at one time or another, had had their own productions. Yet even these titans of the industry had failed to endure.

Day after day I searched my brain for a format which might keep a show on the air. The previous programs hadn't been dull; they simply hadn't attracted an audience large enough to bring a rating satisfactory to the sponsors. No sports show had been able to obtain a survival rating unless it was play-by-play football or baseball or something else in the action category. A plain fifteen minute sports program seemed doomed before it ever hit the air.

Finally I struck on a plan which was to bring me the plaudits of the multitude along with, unfortunately, the scorn of a few.

I decided on a show which would deal in stories with an O. Henry twist; stories set to music, and fableized and dramatized so that they would appeal to the housewife as well as the sports-hungry husband.

Working feverishly, I wrote the first few scripts and worked out a once-a-week format for a fifteen-minute show which would open with a dramatic story, provide a guest interview with a celebrity in which I would work in some sports connection, and then close with another melodramatic vignette.

There was no great concern in my mind as to whether the stories related to sports figures. In planning my scripts I used names which were headline news, as long as there was a touching or stirring anecdote involved. If I could find no athletic connection I merely managed one by asserting that the person concerned had dreamed of being a jockey, a football player, an ice skater, or a baseball star, as the case might seem.

To NBC this was not a sports show and many of the powers that be argued against it, wanting no part of it. But Colgate did want it, seeing in it unlimited audience possibilities, and we put the first one on the air in October, 1939.

The response was instantaneous and utterly satisfying. The show was an immediate smash hit.

As I had feared during the course of my research, there simply weren't enough dramatic sports stories available. I needed two a week which hadn't been told anywhere else. There were hundreds of diligent sportswriters in the nation who daily had made it a business over the years to tell the inside tales of sports as well as to report the straight news. Certainly I had no magic wand which would enable me to come up with constant exclusives of the type I needed.

Then the thought occurred to me that in movies of people whose stories lack dramatic elements the scenarios are "dressed up" to provide a punch. This is done constantly and with unrestrained imagination. In the theater it is known as dramatic license.

Some magazines, particularly those catering to the motion picture trade, use the same technique without any repercussions whatsoever. Their forte is entertainment.

So, too, in my mind, was this show of mine.

I proceeded therefore to use those same techniques. I might also add that invariably I cleared the text of the altered or elaborated story with the person involved, if he or she were living. In cases where the subjects were deceased, certainly no one was being injured. And who can deny that the mantle of imagery, which often is used to cloak dull, drab lives, has been used freely down through the ages to add dash and vigor to even the most herioc of historical figures?

I am certain that no harm ever was done to anyone through our recounting of these admittedly dramatized stories, which were aimed solely at entertaining those who listened to my show.

Yet some sports reporters, angered at my toying with the basic facts which they treated—and rightfully so—as a religious tenet of their trade and aggrieved at my audacity in maneuvering lightly their accepted essentials of time and place, reviled me with their typewriters.

However, I cannot state too emphatically that I was living in the make-believe world of the theater and the license I took was basically harmless. Diversion was my stock in trade and I thrived, rightfully or not, on the same fanciful principles used by other communications media which lift audiences out of a humdrum, monotonous existence of mundane fact and insipid incident.

One of those who to a great extent saw it from my point of view was Ed Danforth, the sage former sports columnist of the *Atlanta Journal*. In his column, "An Ear To The Ground," he wrote:

> January 12, 1943
>
> This department would no more undertake to correct one of Bill Stern's sports broadcasts than it would to try to straighten out Al Capp on details of an adventure of "Li'l Abner." Both features are creations of artists in fiction.
>
> Stern has the most popular sports program on the air. He deals in the dramatic episodes, the heart-throbs of sports and brings to the microphone notable histrionic talents. Only envious rivals say he hams it up.

> Stern is courageous. Where the dull facts of an incident lack warmth, Bill supplies the deficiency. Other commentators cravenly follow the fetish of accuracy and are as dull as record books. Bill dares to breathe the warmth of humanity, of curious coincidence and melodramatic setting into a commonplace incident and leaves his hearers in an emotional glow. Other commentators are stuffy about facts. Bill sifts the facts, discarding tasteless details and substituting pure fancy.

This was the keynote of many complimentary reviews and stories about the show which, as I said, boomed fantastically and shortly earned a rating more dazzling than I had dared expect. We surged ahead of Lowell Thomas and many other such fine shows on the air. At one point our rating was a stratospheric 13.5 which, for a fifteen-minute show, was second only to Walter Winchell. In the field of radio sports this was unheard of, for no sports show ever had advanced beyond a rating of 2 or 3. We were proud of the rating and scratched furiously to keep it up there.

A small number of newspapermen, however, were not inclined to be charitable, if you will, toward our stories. I was flayed and castigated, mostly by a few New York writers. Throughout my later life I always tried to hide my feelings as well as possible under a mannerly exterior of forced calm. But never will I forget the alternating waves of shame, embarrassment, outrage, and anger which swept over me on the occasions when my detractors whipped out their skinning knives and went lustily to work.

One of my most severe critics was John Crosby, Radio and Television editor of the New York *Herald Tribune*. Crosby, an adept and able writer, derided me as a man who "created his own little world of sportsdom, where every man is a Frank Merriwell, every touchdown an epic feat of arms, and coincidence stretches like a rubber band to fit every conceivable situation."

Professionally, disparagement such as this left me unscathed. For, as Crosby admitted in one of the columns in which he again wielded a razor-sharp scalpel on the Stern hide, his essay was written: "Because of widespread public demand—we were inundated by two letters."

A damning torrent, indeed. And further, after outlining the fallacies in some of my stories, he recognized publicly that the people involved were neither being harmed nor were reluctant to appear on the show when he wrote:

> In spite of the malarkey Stern tells about them, athletes are only too happy to appear on his program. This is understandable because, while the truth gets badly mangled, the athletes themselves invariably are cast in heroic dimensions. On his twelfth anniversary program, guests (by transcription of earlier programs) included Babe Ruth, Eleanor Roosevelt, Joe Louis, Bobby Jones, Sonja Henie, Jack Dempsey, Mickey Rooney, Jack Benny, Mrs. Knute Rockne, Eddie Cantor and Herbert Hoover.

It was in my personal associations with other broadcasters and newspaper people that, underneath what I hoped was an undisturbed exterior, I was miserably upset by these criticisms.

In addition to my increasingly despairing battle against drugs, I now felt with morose agitation the whispers of ridicule and derision which went on behind my back whenever I entered a public place where the sports world gathered. I cringed inside whenever I thought of one line which Crosby had written in a passage seared into my mind, ". . . you can start an argument in any saloon where sportswriters congregate by picking out any Stern story as the weirdest he has ever told."

In my worsening physical and mental condition assertions such as these were a knout which flogged me mercilessly, bruising me to the very soul. As does anyone, I desired the respect and acceptance of my fellow craftsmen. Was this such a terrible thing which I was doing, I shouted over and over to myself? Would they do the same with the stakes so large? I hadn't thrown any rocks, yet there was no question that I lived in a house of very fragile glass. The whispers became a tornado which threatened to sweep me out of my mind.

I remember the exultation with which on one occasion when Walter Winchell was going on a vacation I leaped at the proffered opportunity to write a guest column for him. I wasn't the only one making mistakes, I told myself, and I labored long and diligently to unearth the errors of others as a sop to my flagellated pride.

It is indicative of my innermost thinking, more bitter even than I was conscious of at the time, that I titled it "Sure We Make Mistakes." It came out in the New York *Mirror,* and all of Walter's many other syndicated newspapers, like this:

August 23, 1942

Sure, we make mistakes . . . don't you? Radio is a business where mistakes are costly, sometimes funny. Announcers don't always mean what they say. For instance, on the "Martha Jane" show recently, the local lad let go with, "Martha Jane will be back on the air tomorrow with the new babies that have arrived courtesy of Ramsey's Department Store". . . . And the blurb Jack Frasier, NBC announcer, let fly in a late Army recruiting plug, "Don't forget, men, put your name on a penny post card before you forget it". . . . Or maybe you like this one voiced by Sam Hayes, announcing for pancake and waffle flour, "Every time you have company they stick to the waffle iron". . . . Bob Elson is one of America's top sports announcers yet Bob let fly with "It's printed in clear tripe easy to read". . . . Or the time Ken Carpenter turned red, when he heard himself saying "J. P. Watertown, horse dealer, will stand behind every horse he sells". . . . Don Wilson likes to forget the time he stated "Now ladies I will climb up on the fire escape to get a better view. I will hold on with one hand and talk with the other". . . . And we mustn't forget the one Graham McNamee once used on the O'Sullivan Heel program, "O'Sullivan has been the outstanding heel for years". . . . We could go on and on. Want more?

It was Andre Baruch who, on the "American Album of Familiar Music" stated, "When you have a headache ask for it by its full name". . . . Or Fletcher Wiley's "Franco-American spaghetti contains a rich, creamy sauce that few people can eat". . . . Or Ben Grauer's immortal crack, "Go to the Plaza Theater where the feature is 'The Vanishing Virgin'—er—I mean 'Virginian' ". . . . Or Everett Mitchell announcing on the "Farm and Home Hour" when he said "Fertilizer has twice as much organic matter in it—now there's something to sink your teeth into". . . . Or Milton Cross in his never to be forgotten "A & P Gypsy Show" stating "You will now listen to the music of the A & P Pipsies". . . . And we mustn't forget Harry Von Zell who introduced the then President of the United States by saying "Now I present the President of the United States—Heever Herbert, I mean Hoobert Heever, aw nuts, Herbert Hoover!"

But announcers aren't the only ones who make mistakes in radio . . . For instance, the time "Amos and Andy" got twisted in a commercial being done by Bill Hay, who said, "The rich tomato sauce, the pork and beans, are all half-baked—how about your family?" . . . Or the day when the late Lou Gehrig was guesting on a beer show and closed by saying "Fill up your glass with Bupperts reer." . . . But then guest stars have made more than one bull. . . . Max Baer in

> the middle of a heavyweight championship fight leaned over the ropes and yelled down at Clem McCarthy who was broadcasting the fight: "Hey Clem, take it easy, I can't keep up with you." . . . Or, for that matter, the night Sam Taub in describing another fight excitedly yelled into the mike: "He hit him in a neutral corner where it don't hurt". . . . Or maybe you like the one Harriet Hilliard pulled last season on the Red Skelton show: "This is the best bed George Slepington washed in". . . .
>
> News commentators have had their troubles, too . . . H. V. Kaltenborn gets credit for this one: "I'll be back on Monday with the same sad news". . . . Or perhaps you'd care for the one Fulton Lewis, Jr., let fly. Said Mr. Lewis: "Remember Bar Harbor!" . . . Or the day Raymond Gram Swing announced, "The bill was sent by airplane to President Roosevelt who was fishing in Florida waters for his signature". . . . Or the night George Putnam wound up his evening news show with the soap suds commercial "It burps into snuds."
>
> Sure we make mistakes but as I said before don't you? And lest you think yours truly is immune to the error department let me briefly call back to your mind one I pulled which caused me no end of embarrassment. I was describing the Army-Notre Dame football game when for no reason at all I said "Bertelli of Notre Dame is forced out of bounds by a whole group of Army ticklers."

I sweated many hours over this substitute column for Winchell. However faint, it gave me an opportunity to raise a voice of protest against a mental crucifixion which I considered to be without just cause. All too many people were willing to nail me to the mast, to criticize me publicly and privately, adding, unwittingly or not, to my self-induced misery and general despondency.

Even now I do not believe that I would change such a

winning format, not because of derision or mockery, certainly. Without belaboring a point, I can't emphasize too greatly my feeling that this show was strictly entertainment, and being such was one in which I was entitled to unlimited dramatic license.

Someone once coined a line concerning a financially successful person who grieved over the personal disfavor in which he was held, describing him as a man who "wept all the way to the bank." This, in essence, was my own condition throughout this period; an era of personal frustration and professional ridicule, earthly riches and psychological rags, all compounded in growing wretchedness at the ever-tightening hold which drugs were fastening on me. Yet I was making money; big money.

As a young man graduating from college I had seen my family plummet from wealth to the border of poverty. When I began the Colgate show in 1939 I was earning seventy-five dollars a week as an NBC staff member. Putting the Colgate show across jumped me to two hundred and fifty a week and inside of a year this show alone was bringing me four hundred and twenty-five a week. Year by year this Colgate salary climbed . . . five hundred . . . seven hundred and fifty . . . nine hundred . . . a thousand . . . and on up to eighteen hundred dollars a week.

By this time, of course, I had acquired agents, business managers, publicity men, and a staff of writers. With my rating up in the clouds, as time came to renew my contract with Colgate, all of my advisers, official and voluntary, told me to demand three thousand. I was prepared to ask for this figure when I went into a meeting with Stuart Sherman but he knocked the props out from under me with an opening offer of twenty-five hundred a week. I took it, happily.

My new contract boosted the over-all cost of the show up

to forty-three hundred dollars a week, a staggering sum for a fifteen-minute radio program. The reason for this extravagant total was that production costs amounted to another eighteen hundred a week. This added sum was to pay the Colgate quartet which sang the theme song that put us on and took us off the air, as well as to provide background music, writers, producer, director, actors, actresses, engineers, and other personnel.

This show had become my long-awaited chance to earn, and to keep earning, a high income, and I slaved over it as I seldom have worked before or since. I fretted about it constantly, from the time we left the air on one Friday night until we went on the air the following Friday night.

Every word on the show was set to original music which had to be scored for either the organ, the guitar, or the violin and always for four voices. It was grueling, tedious work and we rehearsed a total of from eight to twelve hours, polishing every syllable which was spoken over the air. It was an inordinate amount of rehearsing and preparation which I shouldered, the responsibility being totally mine, and in the interim I still carried on my other spot assignments for NBC.

In addition to whatever else I was broadcasting, whether it was football, track, tennis, golf, or some other event, my Friday night show had to be ready to roll smoothly every week. Since major sports events are on Saturdays the weekends were particularly hectic.

Adding to the complications, the Colgate show had to be put on from all over the country, wherever I happened to be for a sports event. As an example, if I was broadcasting the Masters golf tournament from Augusta, Georgia, an additional problem would be to locate actors and actresses who did not have Southern accents. In Augusta this takes a bit of doing.

Engineering facilities also often were inadequate in some of the smaller towns which weren't equipped to handle network shows. Then, too, although this was not an audience show, on frequent occasions tickets had been distributed by the local station to listeners who wanted to watch the program being put on the air. Spontaneous applause, in such cases, often ruined dramatic effects.

Nonetheless there were times when we couldn't avoid working before an audience. One show I remember particularly well was at Hartford. There was no large auditorium available and those who were making the arrangements had rented a vast cow barn. We put on the show there before some four thousand persons.

It is extremely difficult for someone who has not been in the radio field to appreciate the inner fear, which somehow grows larger and larger as the years march past, that you will say something wrong over the air. This unnerving phantom, ever hovering in the background of your mind, is complicated by the erroneous tips and the human errors that creep into one's analysis and judgment of the news. One of the worst situations into which I plunged came in the fall of 1944.

The St. Louis Browns were leading in the American League pennant race and I was in Detroit that weekend for a Michigan football game. The Friday morning of my Colgate show I telephoned to my office in New York to find out if there was anything "hot." One of my assistants informed me that a weekly known as *Collyer's Eye,* essentially a racing paper, had headlined a purported exclusive that if the Browns lost the pennant there would be an official investigation.

I was stupid. The item had no foundation in fact, but without checking any of the proper baseball sources I went on the air that night and announced, "Attention America: If the St. Louis Browns blow the American League pennant there will be a baseball investigation, according to *Collyer's Eye*."

I added that this was the sheet which had broken the Black Sox scandal of 1919. The editorial inference was that the Browns would be suspected of throwing games.

The reaction was immediate and violent. In St. Louis I was hanged in effigy. J. G. Taylor Spink, publisher of *Sporting News,* the baseball Bible, made a scathing denouncement from home plate in Sportsman's Park, St. Louis. Baseball writers across the country landed on me with both feet. It was a blistering barrage from all quarters which convinced me, once and for all, that baseball is as inviolable as mother love.

Once again I had alienated the newspapermen because of my desire to be there "fustest with the mostest."

Yet, at the height of this furor, there was one heart-warming incident which made me think more highly than I ever had of Ted Husing. The man who was my most bitter rival and who often cut me cold, telephoned and there was a surprising warmth in his voice.

"Bill, I've been through things like this several times myself and I know you're going through hell," he said. "You know, I once called Barry Wood of Harvard 'putrid' and said that the team was 'lousy' and I was barred from their stadium. I know it hurts, but take it easy and it will all blow over."

I was so grateful for his call that my voice choked with emotion. "All I can say, Ted," I gulped, "is thanks for calling."

I wasn't too certain just where the repercussions would end and with what consequences. But in my heart there was an even greater admiration, as well as a new-found warmth, for this dapper man with the city folks' exterior and the home folks' heart.

As he had predicted, it all did blow over, lost in the constantly fresh shuffle of the news. And throughout the next four years I rode the crest of the business wave.

In addition to the twenty-five hundred dollars a week I was receiving from the Colgate show I had my salary as Sports Director of NBC, a post I had taken over in 1940 after organizing the sports department, plus all my other activities such as motion pictures, endorsements, guest appearances, and, with the coming of television, a lucrative move in that direction. Through most of these years I was earning as much as five thousand a week.

Television, as well as my own physical condition, began to make inroads on what was a fabulous income for me after 1948. The following year, 1949, when many radio shows were being canceled, my Colgate salary was cut back to eighteen hundred. Then, as television began to make giant strides and my rating dropped relentlessly, from a slipping 10 all the way down to a minuscule 2, we were finished.

Thus, in 1951, after more than twelve incredible years, Colgate dropped the show.

Chapter 11

Here a star, and there
a star.
—Emily Dickinson

THERE HAD BEEN during the exciting years of its existence a seemingly endless array of famed personalities on the Colgate show. The backbone was a constant parade of sports stars yet we also presented famous beauties, Hollywood celebrities, religious and public figures, entertainment headliners, and notables from the music world.

I came to know a considerable number of these people intimately, and as they pass in review it occurs to me that much of greatness in any walk of life stems from gentleness, humility, and warm-heartedness, qualities I found in so many of them.

Our first guest star in 1939 was Babe Ruth, the immortal home run hitter of the New York Yankees, who had finished his baseball career just a year earlier as a coach with the Brooklyn Dodgers.

The Babe hoped desperately at the time of our first get-together that somewhere in its organization baseball would find a spot for him and I remember the bright optimism of this friendly, hulking man with the projecting personality. I found him easy to work with, showing none of the temperament against which I had been cautioned. He was a boy at heart, never changing in that facet of his character, as he appeared with me again and again through the years until his death on August 16, 1948.

But as he neared the end, the Babe was a man with blasted dreams, a broken-hearted castoff who knew at last that the call he awaited would never come. And in my friendship for him I felt icy anger at baseball's businessmen for never finding him the position he craved with such pathetic eagerness.

Early in the tenure of the program *Look* magazine called me and said they wanted to do a story about a young actress which was to be titled, "Linda Darnell Goes To A Football Game." I agreed to take this starlet with me for my broadcast of the Navy-Notre Dame game in Baltimore. When I met her I knew immediately that she was a sweet, sincere person and we forged one of those spontaneous friendships which has lasted through the years. Since then I have visited her many times at her home in California, consoled her through the breakup of two marriages, and considered her one of the best friends I have in the world. She is not only a fine actress but also a completely lovely person.

We still laugh over a train trip we made together from California to New York in 1949. Our compartments were at opposite ends of the same car, and the night before arriving in Chicago we sat up late playing cards and talking. It was almost daybreak before we finally went our separate ways.

It was quite early in the morning when the train arrived

in Chicago but a group of reporters boarded the train to interview Linda, and somehow were directed to my compartment by mistake. I was awakened by an insistent knocking on the door.

"What is it?" I asked in sleepy annoyance.

"We want to interview Linda Darnell," a voice answered.

"Go away," I said foggily. "She's asleep."

There was a dead silence on the other side of the door and only then did I realize the inference in my statement. Hastily I scrambled out of bed, opened the door, and explained that she was asleep—in her own compartment.

Betty Grable, too, was quite easy to work with before the mike, and yet this beautiful, talented woman who was to go so far in the entertainment world never seemed able to believe that she was as good as her gifts proved her to be.

We also became very good friends, and when Harriet and I prepared to go to California in 1941 to broadcast the Rose Bowl game I wrote Betty and asked her to have dinner with me, forgetting to add that Harriet also would be there.

Betty wrote back that she had become a steady twosome but that they would be glad to make it a threesome on my arrival. That's how I met George Raft. George and I hit it off immediately, for he was a rabid sports fan, and strangely enough was another star who privately had a poor opinion of his own acting ability. We got along so well that frequently, as the years went by, I became his house guest when I was in California.

Famous names provided the panoply for my show: Brash, irrepressible Leo Durocher with his raucous amiability; tennis ace Bill Tilden, who considered himself a magnificent Shakespearian actor but actually was quite hammy; Lucille Ball and her infectious sense of humor; Jack Benny, with his unequaled sense of timing which turned a funny line into a sidesplitting one; the ear-soothing Andrews sisters; reserved and aloof Bobby Jones; boistrous, back-slapping Jack Dempsey, always the champion; the "Lone Ranger," complete with mask and six guns to "get me in the proper mood"; Pat O'Brien, filming *Knute Rockne of Notre Dame* and living the role even off the set; and bashful, lanky Jimmy Stewart, a great Princeton rooter and the most modest man I've ever known.

Early in my football broadcasting days with NBC I went to Nashville, Tennessee, to air a Vanderbilt game. While I was there a petite teen-ager asked me to listen to her sing over the local radio station that night. "I want to come to New York," she said enthusiastically. "I'd like to know whether you think I'm any good."

The next day before the game she appeared at the NBC booth. "Did you listen to me sing?" she asked breathlessly. "Did you think I was good?"

I nodded. "Yes, and I do think you're good. But I also think you had better stay right here with your folks because New York City is an awfully rough place to get a start."

Fortunately, she didn't pay any heed to my advice. It was a couple of years later before I saw her again. Then, just before Christmas, I met her quite by accident. She was truly despondent.

"I've been singing on a local station here in New York and I've just lost the job," she said sadly. "I've refused to accept any help from home because I'm determined to make my own way but I'm pretty near ready to throw in the sponge. Bill," she added plaintively, "could you use me on your show?"

I had to turn her down even though I yearned to give her a lift, because the format of the Colgate show called for nationally known personalities. Several times after that I met her in the corridors at NBC. Always she was still trying and still smiling. And always she asked me the same thing: "Bill, can you put me on as a guest?"

In 1948 I went to her with hat in hand, asking her to please honor me by being my guest star. By this time the little girl from Nashville who had struggled so earnestly was a scintillating, much-sought-after star.

"Why of course, Bill," she said. "I'll be glad to."

And Dinah Shore did.

Guy Lombardo was one of my first guest performers and the urbane orchestra leader, who ranked among the world's leading speedboat drivers, cost me a great deal of money. His enthusiasm for yachting caused me to become so interested in boating that I purchased, in expensive succession, a twenty-six foot cabin cruiser which we called *Wee Pete,* after my little son; a thirty-footer we named *Wee Pete II;* and then a forty-three foot cruiser complete right up to the flying bridge, which we dubbed *Mary May* after our elder daughter.

Another of my early guests was beautiful Susan Hayward. This former model had recently returned from several small Hollywood parts and still was fighting her way up toward the stardom in store for her. I was quite startled, when as we chatted on this first of many visits she said firmly, "Bill, I'm going to win the Academy Award before I'm through."

For once I was tongue-tied. Susan was a young actress, barely starting her motion picture career, and nobody was quite certain at this stage whether she could act or not. And here she was already laying claim to the most coveted acting award in the business.

Susan's steadfast faith in her own ability was not unfounded. Five times she has been in the final balloting for Hollywood's Oscar.

It was an immeasurable personal thrill to me, a moment of extreme happiness for a valued friend's well-deserved good fortune when Susan finally had her long-ago prediction come true. She won the little gold man in 1959 for her superb performance in *I Want To Live*. Her long overdue triumph stands out as a testimonial to the driving determination and unflagging belief which caused her to predict this royal recognition even when she was unknown.

One of my earliest vacation reliefs was a paper-thin young singer by the name of Frank Sinatra. He had been a guest on the show, and as one of the actors in a skit which we were presenting displayed fine acting talent. He had done so well dramatically and was such a great sports fan that I arranged for him to take over in my absence. Sinatra was sensational, but as the movies proved later he is a man of many talents and acting wasn't the least of them.

Also among those who appeared with me was Constance Bennett. In the course of preparing for the broadcast I asked her if she knew anything about sports.

"Of course," she smiled winsomely. "I played basketball."

"What position did you play?" I inquired.

"Captain," she dimpled me to a dead halt.

"Well," I replied lamely, "I guess we'd concentrate on the theater."

Jack Benny's priceless timing made a howling hit of a program I did from London, while covering the 1948 Olympic Games.

During that period of the games, Benny was doing a show at the Paladium. When I sought him out both he and Phil Harris graciously agreed to take the time to appear with me, for a show to be beamed back to the United States.

The hilarious highlight came when we claimed the Olympic one hundred meter sprint championship for the bibulous-acting Harris.

I can remember only one line from that rollicking session

and, possibly, it doesn't read too humorously. But it put everyone in stitches when Benny drawled, "Phil has to be the champion because nobody could beat him if you put a bottle at the finish line."

I shall never, however, forget my first—and later—impressions of Lena Horne. When she came to the rehearsal she appeared quite cool and distant, and because of my great admiration for her talent I stood somewhat in awe of her. After the show I suggested that we all go over to my apartment for a buffet supper which Harriet had prepared and I happened to mention that we had a mammoth set of electric trains set up in the living room for the children.

Dignified and impersonal Lena Horne sat on the living room floor until the wee hours of the morning, playing with those trains as delightedly as a child. I came to know and admire her as a fine person as well as one of the great ladies of show business.

The only guest who failed to appear on time during the more than twelve years of the program was Larry MacPhail, at that time president of the Brooklyn Dodgers. We always arranged to have our guests on hand an hour before we went on the air so that we could have a final rehearsal. But when only fifteen minutes remained until air time and MacPhail still had not appeared, I began searching frantically through the other NBC studios for a possible substitute. As I peered into one studio there, fortunately, Milton Berle was busily engaged rehearsing his own approaching show. Breathlessly I told him of my predicament.

"C'mon, kid," he laughed. "Let's you and me go do that show."

We did. As we finished, MacPhail arrived and explained contritely that he had been stuck in traffic on the Brooklyn Bridge.

The Colgate Newsreel also brought me into contact on several occasions with the hardest working man I've ever known, Eddie Cantor. He was the only guest I ever had who insisted on writing his own interview. Cantor knew exactly what he wanted to say and how he wanted to say it. I found Eddie, like most comedians, to be a very serious, businesslike person off the stage.

Probably the most unusual interview I ever did was with Tommy Dorsey, long a grand friend of mine, in which he replied to every question I put to him with a completely understandable answer—on the trombone. The big, laughing man could really make that instrument talk. His brother, Jimmy, also was a frequent guest and we nicknamed him "Speedy," which later caught on generally because he was always late for rehearsal.

Mickey Rooney staged one of his greatest acting performances just for me. As a publicity buildup we went to the horse races at Santa Anita and the cameraman between races asked Mickey to pretend that he was watching one of his selections come down the stretch to victory. People standing around us at the track went into stitches at Mickey's mugging. It was a real Academy Award performance which convinced me right there of his artistry.

Captain Eddie Rickenbacker, in his several guest shots on the show, most typified to me those admirable traits of tenacity, integrity, and forcefulness. Whenever I think of him I recall the fact that during World War II, when he was lost for twenty-one days in the Pacific, the headwaiter in the Radio City restaurant at which Eddie always ate never would permit anyone else to sit at Eddie's usual table. Even after Eddie was given up for dead that table still was reserved for him daily. The headwaiter didn't even show surprise when word came that Rickenbacker had been found alive.

"You can't kill a man like the Captain," he shrugged.

Yet without question, to my mind the greatest man I've ever known was the Msgr. Rt. Rev. E. J. Flanagan, known simply to all as Father Flanagan and the man who founded the famous Boys Town in Nebraska.

My first meeting with him was early in 1946 while I was in Denver to broadcast the National Amateur Athletic Union's basketball championships and I asked him to make an appearance on my show. Afterward, and quite late at night, we went to my hotel room and without thinking that it was Friday I ordered some ham sandwiches sent up for us. It was only after we had each eaten two or three of them that I realized my mistake.

"Father," I apologized, "I'm terribly sorry. I forgot that this was Friday."

Father Flanagan grinned and patted me on the shoulder. "Forget it, Bill," he smiled. "I forgive you, and I'm sure that the Lord will forgive both of us."

I knew after just a short time in his company that here was an extremely warm and human and yet an absolutely immortal man. This was brought home to me with even greater force that June when, at his request, I went to Boys Town to speak at the annual commencement exercises.

That day is etched deeply in my memory and I shall never forget the admiration which those in the hierarchy of the church, in attendance for the exercises, showed for him. They all loved him and joked with him and there was a great deal of ribbing about his propensity for making a two-dollar wager on a horse race. Father Flanagan just grinned and grinned.

Nor shall I ever forget the adoration and reverence on the faces of those once-homeless kids as they looked up at him while he was handing them their diplomas, fondly calling each one by name. Their faces glowed with an inner light, and it came over me that here without question was a man for the ages.

The most beautiful love affair I ever was privileged to witness through these years was that between tomboyish Babe Didrickson and burly, bent-eared George Zaharias, billed in the wrestling world as "the weeping Greek from Cripple Creek."

The Babe was the greatest woman athlete of them all: slat-thin, stringy-muscled, jut-jawed, and muscularly more proficient in sports than most men. George was a behemoth who could have thrown her over the moon without drawing a deep breath. Yet she controlled with her little finger this massive, rugged, and adoring mountain of a man.

They could have run Romeo and Juliet a dead heat any day of the week.

As for the courtliest gentleman of them all, that accolade, in my mind, must go to Kay Kyser, who gave up fame when he had made his fortune to spend the never-to-be-regained years with his lovely wife and their children.

"I have no interest in returning to show business," Kay told me when I visited them at their home in Chapel Hill back in his native North Carolina. "I have my family and we are extremely contented. There is no substitute, nothing more for which I could wish."

It was to take me many miserable years to realize the profound wisdom of his psychology.

Chapter 12

I climbed and,
step by step, O Lord,
Ascended into Hell.
—William Henry Davies

A SHATTERING PSYCHOLOGICAL CRISIS arose in my life in 1952 when the top brass at NBC called me in and advised me that the duties of sports director were going to be taken away from me and that someone else was going to fill this important post.

Actually there was sound reasoning behind this decision, even though I could neither understand it nor accept it at the time. NBC's top executive minds for several years had debated, pro and con, a widely supported theory that whoever was sports director should not be on the air.

It was the considered opinion of many of them that all too frequently there was a conflict of interest, that a sports announcer who also was sports director too often would be inclined to schedule only those events which he was personally interested in broadcasting.

They finally reached a decision on the highest administrative level that the sports director should be a person who was not involved as a performer but who would be interested purely in which events should be covered by the network without any thought as to who should do them.

I was outraged at the decision. After all, I told myself with furious bitterness, I had organized the sports department at NBC and now that it was running smoothly they were casting me aside.

The truth is that I didn't even attempt to see their side of it. Because by this time, and even though I was to stagger through four more years in my ever more hopeless fight against drugs, I was becoming less and less capable of considering anyone but myself.

In retrospect I can realize that I was a mental and physical wreck even at this time, but somehow, despite the fact that I was constantly in the public eye, I managed to conceal my true condition from the world.

No matter how I felt, however, there was nothing I could do to change the situation or to alter the NBC decision once it was made. This, I was told flatly, was the way it was going to be.

The NBC sports directorship was a much sought after position but eventually the field was narrowed down to two men. In view of the fact I would work directly with the man chosen, I was summoned to the executive suite and consulted about my preference. As it developed, I backed a winner. Although in my later sickness I was to feud with him, at the time of the selection I gave my support to Tom Gallery, a former newspaperman I had met occasionally on the West Coast.

Gallery, a tall, heavy-set man with a hearty voice and manner, finally was selected to succeed me as sports director, a post which actually had become a demanding, full-time position in the highly competitive bidding among the networks for major events.

Tom Gallery and I worked together with superficial smoothness and an apparent lack of friction during his early days at NBC, but he had more than his share of troubles with me as the months passed. I was sick, in mind and body. Subconsciously I held it against him that he had taken my job, perversely delighting in any minor deed which might annoy or checkmate him.

At the same time I was rapidly approaching bottom, and my work was suffering correspondingly, although I stubbornly refused to admit it to myself. By now I was requiring several half-grain injections of morphine to satisfy my greedy need and I was visiting the doctor almost daily. This meant more and more sleeping pills at night, if I was to get any rest at all, followed by the rousing effects of Benzedrine when morning at long last crawled through my window.

Complicating factors which drove me on without letup were the leg pains, the occasionally real kidney stone attacks, and my own inner turmoil, all contributing to a private hell from which I saw no escape.

The day came finally in June, 1952, when I found it impossible to continue. It was in the middle of the afternoon and I was lying on a couch in my office in dull-eyed despair, racked by waves of chills and fever, wondering whether I could even find the strength to sit up if it became necessary. I was lolling there in fogbound lethargy, staring vacantly into space, when the door opened and Gallery came in to discuss some broadcasting plans with me.

His words seemed vague and distant, without sense or

meaning, and I didn't move or reply, slumping loosely on the couch while my mind struggled to grasp what it was that he was saying.

Finally Gallery stopped talking and I noticed that he was simply standing there, staring down at me with a puzzled frown on his face. He inspected me silently for several minutes and then, though the words appeared to be coming from a great distance I could detect the sympathy in his voice when he said, "Bill, why don't you go home?"

Clearing my throat and sitting straighter with weary effort which seemed to drain the last of my strength, I nodded slowly. My words were thick and slurred in my own ears. "Yes, Tom, I think I will."

After he left it seemed to take me hours to cross the room to my desk and after an interminable period of waiting, to raise the doctor on the telephone. Almost incoherently I asked him to get someone to drive me home and I finally understood that he would send a male nurse to meet me at the garage where I parked my car.

It was as though I were moving through a bad dream, the kind where you strive mightily but your arms, legs, and body all work at cross purposes in a liquid type of slow motion. In this manner, as a man in a trance, I made my way woodenly to the garage. Acquaintances waved and called hello but I marched mechanically onward as though they hadn't spoken, concentrating my numbed faculties on placing one foot methodically down in front of the other.

Although I didn't know it at the time, not until much later, Gallery meanwhile had returned to his own office and telephoned Harriet.

"Bill is a very sick man," he told her gently. "I don't know what's wrong with him and it's none of my business. But I do know that he needs a lot of attention and a lot of rest and I want you to know that we here at NBC want nothing for him except to have him well."

This was a wonderful gesture by a man who could have made a great deal of trouble for me and didn't, trying instead to be helpful and to let us know that my job was waiting for me whenever I was ready.

All I remember of the rest of that day is the startled look on Harriet's face when the male nurse helped me into the house and my own jumbled thinking that now, at last, something would have to be done, some resolute and decisive action taken.

Realization had come to Harriet, too, for the very first time, of the critical state at which I had arrived. Up until that moment when the male nurse practically carried me into our home she had believed, possibly hoping against hope and refusing to acknowledge the worst, that I could cope with the situation.

Now she knew I couldn't.

Harriet proved herself a woman of courage, meeting the issue squarely and without flinching. She went immediately to a doctor in New York who long had been a friend of the family and sought his advice. There was a look of absolute determination about her when she came home.

"The doctor told me that there isn't a thing anybody in the world can do until *you* want to do something for yourself," she told me firmly and without compromise. "So, Bill, it's up to you to face this thing head-on."

We discussed the problem thoroughly, mincing no words, and decided that there was only one course of action to be taken. I had to voluntarily hospitalize myself and sweat this thing completely out of my system. We didn't delay. Immediately we called a doctor in Westchester County and sought his advice on which institution would be best suited to my needs.

I insisted stoutly that I would be able to get myself straightened out for good if they could only manage somehow to get me off drugs for several weeks. Possibly I even believed this at the time.

The number of institutions which will take a person for a drug "cure" are limited, and because of my pride I absolutely refused to go any place where I might receive the slightest bit of publicity. Finally, the doctor, who knew but little about my type of trouble, located a small, private institution in New England and made arrangements for me to be admitted.

On the day I was to leave, because I hadn't had any drugs, the craving was gnawing at my nerves and burning in my vitals. The doctor came to the house shortly before we left but he ignored my plea for a calming injection and merely sent us on our way.

It was a ride through the bottom levels of Hades. A flaming need for drugs tore at me with merciless fingers. A nervous wreck even before we started, I was almost out of my mind by the time we located the institution in a rundown section of the village after having lost our way several times.

The place itself was a shock, appearing to me as a dilapidated, ramshackle prison. By this time, because of our wanderings, it was late at night, and I was in utter misery from the symptoms of craving which I had come to know so well; the icy, knotted stomach; the chills and fever; the cottony mouth; the violent headache; and the over-all pains, which make you feel as if God had gone away on a vacation.

Harriet parked our car squarely in front of the only door which showed a light and neither of us said a word as we climbed the steps and approached what was to be for me a chamber of horrors.

Nervously we entered a small reception room, uncarpeted and illuminated by a single reading lamp on a tiny desk. Behind it, reading a newspaper, sat a swarthy man in a soiled white doctor's coat. The appearance of the place and its musty odors terrified me, but Harriet clung to my hand, her steady grip giving me strength, while he wrote my name on an admission card and with seeming disinterest sketchily jotted down my case history.

"Leave him to us," he told Harriet with crisp nonchalance. "You might as well go home and come back tomorrow if you like."

Harriet stroked my arm reassuringly. Her voice was tender and tears glistened in the corners of her eyes as she consoled me. "You'll be all right, Bill. Please try to get some rest and I'll be back in the morning."

I wanted her to take me into the protection of her arms. And yet, if she had, I might have bolted from this terrible place and out into the night. Instead she kissed me quickly, murmuring her good-bys.

Then she was gone. I was alone, terror clutching at my throat until I could barely breathe. There was no time to think as the doctor, matter-of-factly, directed me to follow him. For a moment I was unable to move but mustering strength from some untapped source I reluctantly followed him.

The room to which he escorted me was something out of the Dark Ages. A single unmasked electric bulb glowed harshly in the ceiling, the flyspecks on it standing out like bubonic freckles. Heavy screens masked the windows more effectively than bars. Slowly my eyes took in a straight-backed chair, a narrow, cotlike bed, and a bureau with a sliver of a crack running down one side of its mirror which reflected my image, grotesque and unshapely, as in the hall of mirrors at a fun house.

But it was the heat which really got me. It was an exceptionally hot night near the end of June and the windows, streaked and grimy, were nailed in such a diabolic manner that they could be opened only the merest crack.

A person suffering from drug withdrawal, and my skin was crawling by this time, is particularly sensitive to either extreme heat or extreme cold. The heat in this dingy room caused my head to whirl dizzily.

Perfunctorily the doctor ushered me through the door. He pointed casually to the bureau, telling me to stow my things in it, and then abruptly advised me to "get some sleep." Before I could say anything he was gone and I jerked around nervously at the snap of the lock behind him.

Now the perspiration began to drip from me. Frantically I tore off my necktie, and gasping for air pulled the room's only chair close to the crack in the window, squatting there with my nose to it like a hound at a rabbit hole. Only the merest breath of fresh air filtered through and in sudden frenzy I picked up the chair and smashed it repeatedly against the heavy mesh. The wire had been well-made, because while it puckered in spots my battering couldn't reach the windowpanes and I finally collapsed on the bed, exhausted.

However, the disturbance I had created had not gone unnoticed and within a few minutes I heard the lock click loudly and another doctor stood beside me. This one looked cleaner, and anyhow, in his hand was a hypodermic syringe. Competently he gave me the needle and the injection swiftly calmed my hungry nerves.

With that, although I never closed my eyes, somehow I got

through the endless, terrible darkness. But by daybreak the drug began to wear off and I sat staring hopelessly out across a trash-littered yard into the pale dawn, wondering what in the world was going to become of me.

Those first few days were a nightmare as the doctors rapidly cut down on the drugs and tried at the same time to get me off sleeping pills. I couldn't eat and I was so weak that it was a completely exhausting effort to haul myself up off the bed. Unexpected noises startled me into fitful crying spells and only the fact that Harriet visited me faithfully every day forced me, with some undestroyed vestige of pride, to shave uncertainly with a hand which shook and quivered. Her visits gave me the strength to survive the days, but the nights were excruciating, filled with stark terror, during which I buried my head in the pillow and rolled ceaselessly from side to side in pain and anguish.

I thanked God a million times each day for Harriet because only her visits saved me from going completely out of my mind. And I damned her, too, when, after three days of almost unbearable torture, I begged her to take me out of there and she refused. Her lips trembled and tears trickled down her cheeks but she remained firm and unyielding.

"Bill," she cried, holding me close, "we just can't stop trying. You must stick to our plan and keep fighting this thing. If we quit now we're both beaten."

Violently pushing her away I stamped up and down the room, wringing my hands and sobbing aloud. I didn't even feel any shame at my actions. But finally, as she talked to me, alternately begging and demanding, I saw that she was right. I had to fight it out right here and now or this undoubtedly would be my end.

It went this way for almost a week, the nights filled with screaming shadows and the days saved only by Harriet's devotion, until finally the worst of tne craving exhausted itself by its own fury. A great weakness still held me in its grip and I remained extremely nervous, but the grimmest part seemed to have ended.

Both of us were certain that I had it licked when on the tenth day Harriet took me for a drive, and as we returned to the sanitarium after a relaxed day in the sunshine and fresh air I felt better than I had for longer than I could remember. At the end of two weeks we were convinced that all was well and decided after long deliberation that I was far enough along to leave these depressing surroundings.

The truth of it, which neither of us realized, was that I wasn't anywhere near fit enough to have been discharged. The doctors had relented and gone back to giving me all of the sleeping medicine I asked for, fearing that without it I would have a complete nervous breakdown. They also were of the opinion that once they were able to get me off drugs there would be sufficient time in which to tackle the related problem of sleeping pills. This would arrive, this time of ultimate decision, according to their figuring, when I had regained some physical strength. Now I was too nervous, underweight, and run-down and was resting fitfully even with the benefit of sleeping pills.

They never had the opportunity to put their extended plan into effect.

This was because I was a voluntary patient and the ultimate decision as to whether I remained or left was in Harriet's hands and mine. So, after our mutual decision that I was well enough to leave, contrary to the doctors' advice I signed myself out and we planned to spend three recuperative weeks at a fishing resort in Canada where I would be better able to rest and rebound from my ordeal.

This decision to leave was another one of the big mistakes I made.

In addition to the contributive matter of the sleeping pills, I was to learn later, to my mounting sorrow, that you can't take any medicine when you are in such a precarious physical and mental condition. Danger lurks even in a sugar-coated pill, not because of the contents of the pill, but in the weakening effect it has on your mind by giving you a crutch on which to lean. Even by now I hadn't learned that a man must stand alone, by his own strength; even a man with one leg.

Regardless of the consequences, I was discharged and we flew off to Canada. The following three weeks there did me a great deal of good, even though when we first arrived I hardly had the strength to get in or out of a boat unaided. Gradually, breathing the clean fresh air of the Canadian outdoors and soaking up the warm sunshine, my nerves steadied and I also began to eat again with some signs of relish, actually developing an appetite which allowed me to regain some of the weight I had lost in that demon-filled steam bath in New England.

When the time came to return home we were happily confident that I was on the road to full recovery and I was overjoyed to see Harriet bright-eyed and laughing once again.

Filled with brand new hope I returned to work at NBC.

Chapter 13

We are so largely the
playthings of Fate in
our fears. . . . for all of
us our own particular
creature lurks in ambush.
—Hugh Walpole

WEEK FOLLOWED WEEK in swift succession after our return, and while the craving for drugs occasionally rose up hungrily inside of me and I had to wrestle it mightily there was a growing satisfaction in the knowledge that my work improved vastly.

After six weeks, and an over-all period of nearly three months in which I had been without drugs, I was certain that I had conquered the ghastly problem. My mind was sharp, my voice firm and sure again, and I threw myself into the job with vigor.

But at this point, as I drove up the final hill toward what

I thought was full recovery, I suffered another psychological shock with which I was completely unable to cope.

As I was to learn much later, and almost too late, I was simply marking time between one period of disaster and another. Because the sleeping pills still were providing an infernal crutch, another crackup, considering all of the elements involved, was simply a matter of time. Once again, in catastrophe, it was Gallery who was to sustain the brunt of my indignation.

He came to me, as NBC formulated its plans for the approaching football season, and informed me with as much tact as such a situation made possible that in the National Collegiate Athletic Association's sale of that fall's college football games to General Motors they did not want me to do the television.

"You must be joking," I told him sharply.

After all, I had broadcast all of NBC's top games from the time I had joined the network back in 1937.

"It's no joke, Bill," Gallery insisted. "You still can do the games on radio but they don't want you on television. There are some people who just don't like your work, so that's the way it has to be."

I was stunned. After all, my work had improved immeasurably since my return. A number of people had commented about it quite flatteringly. Shock was succeeded quickly by swiftly mounting anger.

My immediate reaction was that Gallery had engineered this slap in the face, even though, in later and more sensible years, I have regained the analytic ability to realize that it wasn't his doing at all.

Then, too, the thought slashed through my mind that the old prejudices which I so often suspected were at work, and rage gripped me until my hands shook, subsiding only to be replaced by aching bitterness. Moodily I stalked out of the studio and going to a nearby bar, something I seldom ever did when I was alone, ordered a drink.

It was flat and tasteless. I needed something with more lift to it than this.

The visit to the bar, it came to me later, actually had been nothing but a sham, a camouflage for my hidden hunger.

I knew what I needed and wanted; what my limping senses required to give me that old feeling of buoyant confidence and the to-hell-with-it attitude I required so terribly at this moment of frustration. The blow to pride would have been great for any man to handle alone, but in my insecure condition there was more to it than that.

Getting my car from the garage, I drove uptown, gripping the steering wheel until I thought either my fingers or the wheel would have to snap. I drove for hours, around and around the city, but ever closer and closer to the office where, I thought grimly, waited that leering little man with the ready hypodermic syringe.

Darkness had fallen by the time my apparently aimless but inwardly purposeful driving brought me to the block which had been my psychic destination. Slowly I passed the house, keeping my eyes away from it as with some fragment of will power I forced myself to continue. Time and again I drove around the block, a dozen times or more, on each circuit passing that spider's den more and more slowly.

Finally I nosed the car into the curb in front of the building.

The minutes ticked away as I sat there, trying desperately to start the motor and drive away. I couldn't do it. Sweat stood out on my forehead, running down my temples in rivulets. My shirt, soaking wet, clung to my body, and I licked lips which were dry as dust.

Then I panted up the steps and rang the bell.

He opened the door himself, smiling quizzically. "Well, Bill," he said, "where have you been keeping yourself?"

"I've got a kidney pain," I growled, brushing past him.

He smiled even more widely. "I know," he replied. "I know."

This is the only time, I promised myself silently as I paid him, bid him an abrupt good-by, and shouldered my way out into a night which did not look as black as before. This one I had really needed, I argued, but there will be no more. I had been off drugs for three months and was certain that one injection was harmless.

The feeling of guilt dropped away from me as I began to feel better.

With that I drove home, finding some plausible excuse to explain my lateness to Harriet.

In the days which followed, that rejection for the television assignment on the college football games, whether by the N.C.A.A. or General Motors or whoever, left a depressive stamp on me.

I did the college games on radio, striving to do a better job than I ever had before. The pay-off came at the end of the season when the Cotton Bowl officials asked expressly that I be assigned to televise their classic from Dallas on January 1, 1953. It was some measure of solace and redemption.

On this game I decided to try a new technique, that of letting the picture carry the descriptive load and merely adding comments or information where necessary. It was a successful formula and drew this satisfying review from Jack Gould in the next day's New York *Times:*

> Bill Stern, the veteran sportscaster, showed a rare brand of both courage and common sense yesterday. Noted for years

as an announcer who practically never stopped talking, he completely altered his technique in giving over the NBC network an account of the Cotton Bowl game between Texas and Tennessee. He was a reporter, not a chattering and artificial expert, and it was an immense improvement.

The contrast between the Stern of yesterday and the Stern of old was so marked—and so welcomed—that there could be no doubt that the sportscaster had deliberately elected to heed the cries of many football fans to let the TV camera tell the story. Bill, who has had his share of criticism from both sports writers and TV critics, deserves credit for making an about-face. For a person in the public eye that is never easy.

The Texas-Tennessee game was an acid test for Mr. Stern because the Cotton Bowl attraction was an incredibly dull one; Tennessee was so inept and awkward on the field that it really was no contest. But whereas in days gone by Mr. Stern would have endeavored to camouflage the obvious with a torrent of words, yesterday he succinctly observed that Tennessee was not very good, and let it go at that.

Indeed, Mr. Stern was disciplining himself so severely that an element of stage fright could be detected over the loudspeaker. He clipped his sentences too sharply and had a tendency to speak in sing-song phrases. But once he gains confidence in his new approach to sportscasting these minor problems should be ironed out. The big problem he licked yesterday.

Mr. Stern's major improvement was that he did not chatter while a play was in progress, for the most part restricting his comment to giving the name of the player who carried the ball. On passes and kicks, which used to find Mr. Stern in a state of virtual frenzy, he kept still and allowed the viewer to see for himself what was happening. Even during several occasions when the teams took time out, he said nothing. The viewers waited along with the spectators of the

> bowl for the game to resume, which is enlightened television.
>
> Similarly, Mr. Stern abstained from analyzing the game in technical gobbledegook, albeit his partner, Joe Hassel, did not. Once he combines more relaxation in his voice with his new economy of words, Mr. Stern should complete successfully the transition from radio to TV. His worst troubles apparently are over.
>
> That not only Mr. Stern is recognizing the need for change in video sportscasting was evidenced by Jim Britt, who reported the Sugar Bowl game between Georgia Tech and Mississippi over ABC. At the close of his broadcast, Mr. Britt asked for the comments of viewers on whether he had talked too much or too little. From the snatches that this viewer heard he seemed to have talked just about right, although occasionally he was rather flowery.
>
> Red Barber, who reported the Orange Bowl game between Alabama and Syracuse, and Mel Allen, who was present at the Rose Bowl game between Southern California and Wisconsin, were two gentlemen still very much enamored of their own words, which, judging from repeated samplings, just flowed on and on and on.

Critical it was and yet eminently fair, I thought, and I wondered sadly what Gould would have thought as he sat in front of his typewriter and wrote about my "element of stage fright" if he knew of my needle weakness. And would he have written that my "worst troubles apparently are over"?

The game had gone extremely well, however, and there was added proof of this when Gallery telephoned me the night after the Cotton Bowl telecast and said, "Congratulations, Bill, that was one of the best jobs you ever did."

It was like pouring water on a duck's back. For by now I had a definite feeling of estrangement bordering on outright hostility whenever I was in Gallery's company, and I finally decided that, at long last, I would leave NBC.

My chance wasn't long in coming. For that spring of 1953 I met Augustus (Gussie) Busch, president of the Anheuser-Busch Brewing Company and owner of the St. Louis Cardinals baseball team in the National League, and he confided to me that he was interested in sponsoring a network sports show. We had several long discussions and I finally obtained from him a firm commitment.

I was bitter enough to decide that I definitely was not going to throw this million dollar prize package into NBC's lap.

Keeping the deal secret, I asked Gallery for my release and he was perfectly willing to give it to me. However, there were those in the executive department who weren't quite so willing to give me up after eighteen years and I finally had to go all the way to David Sarnoff, chairman of the board of RCA which owned NBC.

"We hate to lose you," Sarnoff said in graciously granting my release, "but if that's the way you feel about it, Bill, we certainly won't hold you to your contract."

Hindsight, always better than foresight, has convinced me that it wasn't a particularly wise move. Anything done in anger is wrong, I realize all too fully now, and looking back I find without surprise that the years in between have washed away all of that old bitterness.

Gallery was in a tremendously difficult position and I did nothing to make it easier. NBC, on the other hand, always had meant everything to me and should never have had anything but my admiration and gratitude. Tom Gallery did everything he could to help me and it is my considered opinion that he has made a far better sports director for NBC than I ever did.

But what is finished is written, no matter how heavy the mantle of regret, and it must be recorded that I went to the American Broadcasting Company with that lush Budweiser contract in my pocket.

This was a package which didn't require any selling on my part. Budweiser was committed to a program which would pay the network over which I was broadcasting more than one million dollars.

The result was that I was given a three-year contract by ABC at $55,000 a year guaranteed and the contract from Budweiser alone would net me an additional $125,000. ABC set me up in an office and I went to work doing a daily show for Budweiser and a late evening show on television for a local sponsor.

Throughout these months of upheaval, the tearing up of my deeply-buried roots at NBC, I gradually had begun to return to that accommodating doctor for an inspiring injection. In the early months after that upsetting day at NBC when my football services were rejected for television, I went no more than once a month; sometimes even less.

In the beginning I didn't require much, for my body had been cleansed of drugs and only a little was required to give me the desired effect.

Disgust at my own back-sliding, horror of a repetition of the frightful New England incident, and fear of hurting Harriet were constant checkreins on my appetite.

I fought hard and bitterly as month followed month, but ever so slowly, as a man sinking in a particularly slow-working quicksand, I began to fall back into that same old ruinous rut.

Chapter 14

A dismal universal hiss, the sound
Of public scorn.

—Milton

SOMEONE ONCE OBSERVED that man is the most tenacious of all animals where the matter of clinging to life is concerned and I am inclined to believe that this is so. If not, there is no explaining my survival during those next three years of perdition, years in which I slid lower and lower down the human scale to become a pitiful bag of bones ridden by an appetite for drugs which should without question have killed me.

The load which I attempted to carry would have been great for any man, but it was too much for a man with my few strengths and many weaknesses. My body was a citadel of pain and my mind a morass of fears, doubts, grudges, and blank wanderings. It seems impossible for any human being to have spent more time on the physical and psychological rack and survived.

Those early months after I went over to ABC possibly should have filled me with determination to make a success of this brand new venture and inspired me to take a firmer grip on myself. Yet, in my muddling thinking, I was an enemy in an alien camp. Those with whom I worked were blameless. They attempted to make me feel at home and were considerately helpful. But I had been at NBC for so long that any other place had to be foreign territory.

The needle, with its soothing counterbalance for all the faults I wasn't hardy enough to handle, became the inevitable answer.

Just this once; never again. How many times I said that to myself, even while I knew full well in my heart that this was merely an excuse to justify to myself the dangerous course I was treading. It wasn't often, at first. Once a month, maybe. But then another crisis which I could not handle would arise and the hypodermic syringe was the all-inclusive remedy.

Soon it was twice a month, followed by still another attempt to bring this to a halt before it went completely out of hand. Sometimes, in those early days, I did check those devilish hungers momentarily. Then a new emergency would arise and I was back at it once more.

Now it became twice a month; three times a month; once a week; and, finally, as it had been in the past, a constant and insatiable yearning over which I no longer had the least control.

In some mysterious manner, don't ask me how for I do do not know, I struggled along in seeming normality as the buildup went on for three full years, and I was hooked worse than I ever had been before. Near the end of this period I no longer even tried to fight off the craving. All I knew was that I had to have it, day in and day out, night in and night out.

Another factor was the ease with which I could obtain drugs because I still was having kidney stone attacks and, by now, I was a highly accomplished actor when it came to simulating a seizure. As I have said, even on the road it was no problem to obtain an injection from a strange doctor. Usually I was recommended by people of importance, and as a visiting celebrity I was above suspicion.

But at long last, on January 2, 1956, came my personal Armageddon.

ABC sent me to New Orleans to televise the New Year's Day Sugar Bowl game between the University of Pittsburgh and Georgia Tech, back to New Orleans where nineteen years earlier I had broadcast my first Bowl game. But this was to be a day of shame, disgrace, and utter humiliation.

Our crew arrived in New Orleans three days before the game, which was on January 2 because January 1 was a Sunday, to check over all the arrangements for televising the affair.

The visit opened on an ominous note when, on one of the rare occasions this had happened to me, I had difficulty locating a doctor who would give me an injection. As the first night passed without success I was severely ill. Before I finally did locate a doctor who consented to take care of me I was nauseated and stricken with all those sickening symptoms of craving.

Complaining of my pains and certainly looking ill, I talked the doctor into giving me what actually was an overdose, on the night before the game. Later that night I complicated matters by swallowing what must have been a slight overdose of sleeping pills.

Before going to bed that night, which was the eve of the game, I left a call for seven o'clock in the morning.

From that moment on everything is a bad dream, swathed

in a mist-shrouded cloak somewhere between this world and the next. Vaguely, as something half-remembered, I recall awakening, whether by the call I had asked for or not I cannot tell, and then summoning the doctor who had given me the injection the previous night.

There was no question but what I was in a drugged stupor and the one sharp mental picture I retain is of him refusing at first to give me another injection.

"I have a ball game to televise," I pleaded. "Doctor, this pain is killing me. Just one shot and I'll be able to get through it and get back to my own doctor in New York."

Finally he yielded, and when he had done his job and gone I passed out completely.

However, I did, somehow, remember to leave a call for eleven o'clock with the hotel switchboard and the insistent summons of the telephone finally forced me awake at that time. Merely rising from the bed left me weak and breathless.

Slowly pulling myself together I staggered to the bathroom and shaved as best as I could, hardly able to distinguish my features in the mirror. Then it took me more than an hour to dress myself with fumbling, wooden fingers.

My trip to the stadium was a nightmare in bright sunshine. The brilliance of the day lanced into my eyes, hammering at the back of my skull; and as the taxi crawled along I sat in the back with make-up case on my lap, and without the aid of a mirror daubed my television make-up on my face. I must look, I thought disgustedly, like Pagliacci with a hangover.

Arriving at the stadium, I hurried as rapidly as my condition permitted to the elevator. Waiting there to take me up to the broadcasting booth was Al Wachenheim, a friend of mine who long has been a member of the Sugar Bowl executive committee. If he noticed that anything was wrong Al charitably never said a word, yet I suspect he must have questioned my late arrival and bedraggled appearance.

Hastily I made for the booth, and Billy Whitehouse, ABC sports editor, and Ray Scott, who was to work the game with me, waved in relief as I entered, because never previously had I been this late for an event. There was no time for conversation. A quick glance told me that the rival captains were meeting in the center of the field and that the start of the game was only minutes away.

My fingers were annoyingly stiff and slow as I fumbled over the setting up of my line-up board and I was no more than half ready when I received the cue that I was on the air. The opening lines came of their own volition, simply through the habit of years.

"Good afternoon, ladies and gentlemen. This is Bill Stern speaking from the Sugar Bowl in New Orleans where this afternoon we bring you the Sugar Bowl classic between. . . ."

Between who? My mind struggled to mesh into gear. Then it came, with hardly a perceptible pause.

". . . Pittsburgh and Georgia Tech. The captains are going out on the field and here are the starting lineups."

I looked down at the line-up board, still incompleted, and my eyes picked out the starting list of names in the Pittsburgh line-up.

> For Pittsburgh, at left end, Joe Walton, two hundred and ten pounds, from Beaver Falls, Pennsylvania.
>
> At left tackle, Bob Pollock, six feet, two inches, from Mount Carmel, Pennsylvania.

My head swam. My lips felt puffed, and pronouncing the words seemed like an impossible chore. Blinking my eyes rapidly to clear away the thickening mist before them, I clutched the board for support. Let's see, where was I?

"At left tackle . . ."

No, I had said that; or had I? No, I guess I hadn't. Slowly, fighting to pull myself together, I started again.

"At left tackle, ah, Bob ah . . ."

Bob who? Now where was his name? It had to be somewhere there on the board. But where? Here it was. No, that wasn't it. Wait a second, this was a note. Maybe they wanted me to read this. What did it say?

The words swam in front of my eyes and I stared at the scrawl which a side glance showed me Billy Whitehouse was holding for me to read. I couldn't believe what it said. Why, this was idiotic. Frowning, I read it again but the words didn't change. They still contained that short, terse order: "Give it to Scott."

There was nothing to give to Scott. He already had it and I heard him running with swift urgency through the list of players as the two teams lined up down on the field.

Woodenly I sat there through the kickoff, Scott's voice damning in my ears. I should be the one giving that play-by-play account of the game. What had I done?

Then indignation mounted inside me, succeeded quickly by rage. What right did they have to take me, Bill Stern, off the air? I was handling this game right here in this same stadium when everybody in this booth was either an unknown or a kid in knee pants.

These furious thoughts were interrupted as Whitehouse dropped a hand on my shoulder. "Come on outside, Bill," he said. "I think you ought to have a cup of coffee."

Maybe that would help, I reasoned, forgetting my anger as I concentrated on raising myself with extreme difficulty from my seat and following him out of the booth.

Then the anger rekindled inside me as Billy said, "Bill,

New York just told me to take you off the air and to keep you off."

Nothing like this had ever happened to me before. My pride, as robust as ever despite my condition, was stung. Fury flamed through me and I raged and blustered at Billy. Then, realizing for the first time the dreadful consequences which could follow this appalling incident, I headed in groggy distress for the nearest telephone.

My first call was to Robert E. Kintner, then president of ABC, in New York. Getting him on the wire, I pleaded to be put back on the air. When he said there was nothing he could do I telephoned John Daly, vice-president in charge of news and special events. He, too, informed me that there wasn't anything he could do from that end.

Both of them, of course, had talked to Whitehouse immediately after my debacle and they realized full well that I was in no condition to make the broadcast.

Stubbornly, although I was suffering keenly both in body and soul, I spent most of the afternoon telephoning various executives in New York and failing to reach them because they undoubtedly were dodging any conversation with a man in my obvious disturbed state.

Shortly before the game ended, I realized the utter futility of trying to do anything else as far as this game was concerned. Dejected, sick, humiliated, and filled with consternation as I contemplated what I had done to my career, I walked slowly from the stadium with Whitehouse. I stood there in a daze until he finally managed to locate a taxicab and the silence was broken only once as we rode back to the hotel.

"I'm not sure what you've been doing, Bill," he said hesitantly. "But whatever it is, you'd better get hold of yourself and stop it."

Stricken with shame and illness, I told Whitehouse I would see him in New York and went to my hotel room and locked myself in. For several hours, needing some stimulus, I tried to telephone the doctor who had injected me that morning, but when I finally did manage to get in touch with him he refused to attend me. Meanwhile, I also had been attempting to reach Tommy Velotta, administrative vice-president of ABC and the man in direct supervision of the sports department. It was quite late at night when I finally got him on the phone.

"Bill, I don't want to talk about it," he said abruptly. "You embarrassed all of us today."

"But, Tommy," I cried, "I can't even sleep."

Velotta, who had no idea of my condition and who was aware only that I had disgraced the network, was curtly unsympathetic. "Why didn't you think about that this afternoon?" he countered sharply before hanging up with decisive finality.

Sleep would not come that night, one in which I stumped the floor in almost intolerable pain and anguish. Crushed at this latest turn of events, I finally wore myself down so near to exhaustion with my pacing that I collapsed into a chair and sat for hours staring into space.

Eons later, dawn broke in front of my aching eyes and the room was flooded with sunshine before I realized, as I sat there in a stupor, that I was scheduled to catch an eight o'clock plane for New York. Hurling clothes into my suitcases I raced for the airport but I had missed the plane.

An hour later I was on another plane, but fretting as we made frequent and lengthy stopovers I abandoned it at Charlotte, North Carolina, and for two hundred and fifty dollars hired a charter plane to rush me to New York in an attempt to make my regular broadcast that night.

At this point misfortune played a final card against me. We ran into bad weather, and after a great deal of cloud-covered maneuvering had to head for the Philadelphia airport.

Sitting in the back by myself, shrouded in what seemed to me to be a prophetic darkness I realized that I had missed this show, too. What, I wondered as we broke through the heavy overcast and finally saw the lights of the landing strip beneath us, was to happen to me now?

Chapter 15

The heart of man is the place the devils dwell in: I feel sometimes a hell within myself.

—Sir Thomas Browne

MY HOMECOMING WAS another nightmare. On my arrival, sapped of strength and nearly incoherent with pain and anxiety, I found Harriet so distraught that she could hardly speak.

Her eyes were swollen from weeping, and seeing in her the accumulating wreckage of our life I felt a terrorizing, unconquerable hopelessness. This demon inside me was not only ruining my health and career but, as I had thought so often before, Harriet's happiness and peace of mind as well.

We talked through that night, I pledging over and over again to defeat this monster. Hours later, each one marked and stained by my recriminations and our tears, we decided that our first step was to locate a doctor who knew specifically how to treat this evil.

This we set out to do the very next day and the doctor on whom we settled ordered that I should be attended night and day by male nurses as the drugs were cut off completely.

Yet even this doctor, long familiar with cases such as mine, could not endure the sight of a human being taking the physical beating I went through those next few days. Finally, yielding to my terrible distress, he gave me an injection and suggested that I be moved to Le Roy Hospital, a private institution in New York's East 60's.

Within a week after the catastrophe at New Orleans, I was taken to Le Roy Hospital, and as we entered the vaulted, pine-paneled reception room I doubt if I could have made it without Harriet at my side, her faith and determination giving me strength to go on from one moment to the next.

Once admitted, the doctors there gave it to me cold turkey. Drugs and sleeping medicines were withdrawn immediately and completely.

I almost went insane if, indeed, I wasn't already.

There is no way of describing how I hung on through the first day and into the second. But at the end of two days I was ready to give up.

Spots floated before my eyes. Lights flashed on and off, and strange, grotesque shapes and figures straight from hell crawled over the walls and the bed on which I thrashed and screamed. Twice I attempted to reach the window and hurl myself through it to the street far below, raving that even death was preferable to this unbearable misery. Each time I was restrained by alert attendants.

After four days I was certain that not even life itself could be worth this kind of agony and I determined that the next day I would walk out of this torture chamber no matter what anyone said or did. I was a voluntary patient and I'd be damned eternally if anybody was going to keep me here against my will.

Early the following morning, while I was planning my flight to freedom, a fresh-faced young doctor came into the room, and after introducing himself told me that he was a rabid Oklahoma football fan and wanted to know if I felt up to talking for a while. We talked for more than a half-hour and suddenly, looking me squarely in the eye and placing a steady hand on my arm, he said intensely, "You're planning to leave here, aren't you?"

Angrily I threw aside his hand and my voice was venomous. "You're damned right I am. Nobody could take what I've been going through in here. I've had it."

Unmoved, he eyed me coldly. "If you quit on this thing now," he told me, "I will lose all respect for you. It's not bad being down; the terrible thing is when you quit fighting. If you fold up now nobody can have any respect at all left for you. If you stay here and keep on trying, no matter how tough it is, you'll be fulfilling everything I always thought about Bill Stern."

"Baloney," I snapped sneeringly.

"No, it isn't," he said levelly. "I've read a lot about you. What was it, a bunch of baloney how you lost your leg and still made a success out of yourself? Well, if it wasn't, you've got the guts to make it this time, too."

With that, he stood up and strode out of the room.

For hours I lay there, inspecting myself under a mental microscope. Did I have the guts? I didn't really know and yet he had pricked some last vestige of pride and I knew that I had to try again.

That visit, by a man whose name I can't even remember

but to whom I owe a tremendous debt for instilling me with courage, turned the tide in my favor, at least temporarily.

From that morning forward, although I still was a very sick man, I at least tried to co-operate with those who were attempting to make me well.

Three weeks later they had done as much as they possibly could and I was released. Not that I was a picture of health; indeed I was frightfully weak and run down.

But I was off drugs.

The rocks on which I was to founder, even yet, however, were the sleeping tablets. Once again it was the old, old story of one crutch leading to another. Rest was impossible without sleeping medicine and it had been ordered for me during the latter days in Le Roy Hospital, as it had been in the past, to prevent a complete nervous breakdown. Back home again I resorted to it freely, building up to the point where I was taking as many as sixteen tablets a night in an attempt to obtain rest.

Through three more nerve-shattering weeks I waged an ever-losing battle to stay away from drugs, but after a total of six gruesome weeks I threw in the sponge and surreptitiously visited a doctor for "just one" shot. It was my first step back into the same devilish pit.

Blasphemy my weakness; for I did. Yet all of the soul-searching and personal preaching in the world didn't help. I thought of Harriet and the children and of my career, all disappearing into the cauldron of my appetite. I prayed and I raged violently at myself and this desire.

Then I sought out a doctor.

Harriet knew almost from the first. The haunted look returned to her eyes, eyes which once again were constantly red from weeping. She pleaded with me, alternately begging and threatening, but to no avail.

Meanwhile, and I shall never know how I managed to do it, I continued my daily broadcast. Gradually it became more and more impossible. The voice, of which I had been so proud, became broken and scratchy. My lips would form words but no sounds would issue from my mouth, my face contorting in these lapses as I strove wretchedly to enunciate. Harriet, squirming in agonizing embarrassment and helpless grief, could no longer bear to watch me as I tried to perform.

The mere act of getting out of bed was a problem, my nerves being so frayed and jangled, until I took large doses of sleeping pills even on arising, just to calm myself down. Only then was I able to shave with a shaking hand and make a pretense of going to work. Seldom did I arrive at the studio before two o'clock in the afternoon and there I would struggle for hours to tape record my evening show.

During this period I was doing a fifteen-minute early evening radio show for Allstate Insurance five days of the week, and a five-minute television show from 11:10 to 11:15 P.M. for the network.

The Allstate program was the most expensive radio sports show ever to have gone on the air, with the exception of the old Colgate Sports Newsreel. It was a show which cost in the neighborhood of six thousand dollars a week, a tremendous amount of money for a fifteen-minute radio show in these television days. Our format consisted of commentary on the day's sports news and then cut-ins from around the country for an on-the-scene report from wherever news was breaking: the Soap Box Derby at Akron, Ohio; a major league meeting in Chicago; or a horse race at Hialeah in Florida.

It was this early evening show which became my greatest problem due to the fact that, while I ordinarily had Demerol or Dilaudid on hand to take when I arose in the morning usually washed down with a cup of coffee, I still needed a morphine injection to calm me completely. Many times, for one reason or another, it was impossible for me to obtain this injection before doing the late afternoon show, and on these occasions I had the shaking horrors.

No less than two of these times, Murdock Pemberton, my immediate superior, let me go on the air when I shouldn't have even attempted it, yielding to my pleading insistence that I felt all right.

The first time, complaints from various stations poured into ABC in a flood because my words were so slurred and indistinct that it sounded as though I were completely intoxicated. The low, resonant voice which had been the foundation of my success now was distorted into a high, squeaking pitch in which the words ran together confusingly. The stations criticized ABC lustily for "letting a drunk go on the air."

Pemberton, waving a sheaf of these outspoken complaints, warned me that any recurrence would call for my immediate dismissal.

When it happened a second time, I wasn't quite so bad, and while there were a few complaints at least I wasn't summarily fired. Pemberton let me know in no uncertain terms, however, that one more such incident would mean my end at ABC, this time without fail or recourse.

I knew even prior to this, of course, that I wasn't doing a good, hardly an acceptable, job. Nor was there any question in my mind that the only way to improve my work was to stop taking drugs. Struggle as I would, however, it was no use. I was powerless to conquer that terrible craving.

Eventually it became necessary for me to labor seemingly endless hours even to get my voice to a range where it was faintly acceptable. These were dismal hours in which I passed despairingly from one day to the next without any hope whatsoever of ending this horror-stricken existence.

Life was a round of doctors who injected me to ease the pain of my "kidney stones." Some of them knew I was lying but my self-respect long since had vanished. I didn't care whether or not they thought or knew that I was acting or lying. All that mattered was that I get an injection and I no longer cared what I had to do to get it.

I was hurtling uncontrollably toward the cliff at the end of the road.

Chapter 16

For the world, I count it
not an inn, but an hospital;
and a place not to live, but
to die in.
—Sir Thomas Browne

THE END WASN'T LONG in coming, arriving with cataclysmic finality. By the beginning of June, 1956, it no longer was a question of my work and my home. They long since had failed to have any counter effect on my insatiable appetite for drugs.

By this time the situation was becoming, with increasing rapidity, a matter of life or death. Life appeared a certain loser.

I was down to 135 pounds from a normal weight of 165. I could no longer perform because my lips twitched uncontrollably, my mouth was fever dry, and my throat felt as if I was swallowing razor blades. The words which were my livelihood simply wouldn't come any more.

Every day now I was having an injection and the almost incomprehensible part of it is that I never had to purchase morphine illegally or inject myself. I was, in every sense of the words, a "legal addict." My resultant pitiful condition, mentally as well as physically, had a chain reaction which aggravated my leg and the incessant series of stones forming forever in my kidneys.

No part of my body was without pain from one source or another: the drug miseries which racked mind and flesh; the increasingly intermittent pains in my stump; the violent, piercing agonies as I passed an endless series of kidney stones.

Those unceasing visits to doctors for the relief of the hypodermic syringe weren't all the result of my craving. The anguish of my assorted ailments naturally increased with my weakened condition, and while I could fake the pain whenever necessary, as often as not the suffering from leg and body was a contributive goad to my demands.

Kidney stones are extremely painful, as I have said before, and the drugs relaxed the nervous system so that they could be passed more easily. Yet, in retrospect, the leg was one of the chief culprits. The stump never had healed properly and in the finishing of the protective flap a nerve had been pinched. The annoyance was continual but there were times when excrutiating spasms lanced through the stump for periods of from a week to ten days, without relief.

As my physical condition went from bad to worse my leg and kidneys seemed to come diabolically alive and take on a personality of their own, all aimed at conspiring in my destruction. It was a combination of catastrophe which, without question, spelled my doom.

Harriet, too, was going through a personal hell all her own, distraught and frantic as she attempted again and again to straighten me out and saddled, also, with the added problems of running a home and keeping this dread secret from our children. Increasingly nearer the breaking point, she fought on bravely at my side, refusing with stubborn courage to believe that together we could not defeat this terror.

But finally, early that June, even my long-suffering, indomitable wife was ready to concede that we were lost.

One night, when I came home in an appalling condition, she sat staring at me as I jerked nervously about the room in tigerish torment and then suddenly burst into tears. Sobs racked the slender body which, long since, should have been drained of tears in the frightful uncertainty I had made of her existence. Miserably helpless, I simply stood there until she cried herself out and wiped her swollen eyes.

"Sit down, Bill, and listen to me," she said in a dead, lifeless tone.

Then her voice became firm and decisive, filled with a determination I had never heard before. "I have to tell you this, Bill, and I want you to really understand me."

She paused and her next words seemed to knock the breath from me. "Bill, I can't, no, I won't, take this any longer."

Numbly I fixed my eyes on the floor, trying to evade the misery in her eyes.

"I mean it, Bill," she added relentlessly. "This thing has driven me to the point where you must do something about it, once and for all, or I am going to leave you."

Even in my condition her words were crystal clear. Lose Harriet? Such a possibility, somehow, never had entered my mind. Harriet had always been there, standing beside me sturdily when I needed her. Without her, I realized fully, there would be no today and certainly no tomorrow. Without her I was irrevocably lost.

"Do you understand me, Bill?"

Too well, even though for a few shocked minutes I couldn't locate the raven's croak which substituted for a voice. Convulsively, I swallowed, over and over, envisioning the unbearable thought of her being gone from me. Then the words came, stumbling one over the other between my sobs, as I pleaded a cause which for the moment seemed beyond recall.

Desperately I flung myself down beside her and put my head in her lap. I begged. "Dearest, I'll do anything you say. Anything. Just don't talk about leaving me. Give me one more chance. Just one. I'll do anything you say, but for God's sake don't leave me all alone."

I could feel her compassion as she held me close and yet I knew that Harriet, always before willing to believe that I could conquer this horror, was finished. People who have loved and lived together don't necessarily require words to communicate their thoughts to each other. More than words, this intangible system shouted to me that Harriet had arrived at the point of no return.

It was as if she had read my thoughts. "I'm sorry, Bill. I do love you. But it's simply that I can't possibly go on this way any longer. This time it is completely up to you, and you alone, whatever happens to us. I've done all I can. No, I've done all I will."

We talked for hours, as we had so often in the past, but this time there was a difference. Harriet now remained coldly adamant. At long last she had reached the absolute end of her hope and belief.

"All right," I told her in conclusion, "this time I will beat it. I promise you I will."

There was unyielding finality in her reply. "Bill, this time you'll have to."

We had decided, in the course of our conversation, that a short "cure" certainly couldn't be the answer. We had tried that too often before with dismal, inconclusive results: my first trip to a hospital in Manhattan, in quiet isolation at home, that black hole in New England, and my final farce at Le Roy. This time, if I could accept it, I would be going away for a long time. It was the only way out or, after all the trials and errors of the past, we both knew irrefutably that I would never be cured.

So I called a doctor.

But not, this time, for drugs.

Putting aside my pride, or what remained of it, I told him my story and explained that I wanted the name of an institution which would take me and keep me until I was cured unquestionably, no matter how long a period was involved. There were, he advised me, two places which seemed to fill my requirements. One was in White Plains, New York, and the other in Hartford, Connecticut.

We decided on The Institute Of Living in Hartford and, within a few days, arrangements were made to have me admitted even though they ordinarily did not handle cases such as mine.

It was a beautiful, sunny day, that morning of June 16, 1956, when we started out for Hartford. Before I climbed into the Thunderbird, where Harriet waited at the wheel, I took a large dose of Demerol and I was feeling slightly "high" from it as we drove out our winding driveway and headed for the Merritt Parkway.

Harriet, chin firm and eyes on the road, was very businesslike. This time, I knew, she would not yield short of a complete cure. She had said so again as we prepared to leave home.

"Remember, Bill, this is the end," she told me. "I just won't and can't take it any longer. This is absolutely the last time. You'll have to make it stick—or else."

This time I had to want it desperately enough to make it. This couldn't be another weak effort, a few weeks of uneasy peace and then a gradual slide back into the same old rut.

But could I do it?

Frankly, I had to admit to myself, I didn't know. It was a question which nagged me constantly as Harriet drove in silent preoccupation. What was left to say or to talk about? Actually, nothing. But, as the miles and the Demerol wore away, I began to get more and more uncomfortable. The old questions which up to now had no permanent answers began to haunt me while I shifted in the seat, increasingly tense and irritable.

There were so many problems involved in my condition: the leg which had been the very beginning of it all, the kidney stones, the frustrations and rejections, and the needle-punctured years. My mind was a turmoil as the miles unreeled, vacillating between self-pity and self-scorn.

Harriet's voice shook me out of my long reverie. "There it is, Bill."

We had stopped for a traffic light and she was pointing to the opposite corner. Tall buildings rose up from behind a high brick wall.

"Yes," I replied. "Yes, there it is."

The imminence of my admission to this unknown fortress of fears heightened my nervousness and suddenly I needed a shot desperately. Slumped in the seat, I hugged my arms across my stomach against the swelling, icy knot inside although a trickle of sweat was running down my forehead. I made no attempt to wipe it away, for if I moved my arms, that iceberg in my middle undoubtedly would grow larger.

The car moved ahead, slowly, following the barricade of brick and Harriet braked gently as we came to the wide gates of a driveway. A bronze sign stared back at me, announcing impersonally:

"Institute Of Living."

Harriet swung the car in under the towering elm trees and I inspected the buildings which were to be my prison. Here, once again, wooden-faced, uncaring strangers were going to "make me well." Or try.

I was scared. How many times had I been through this before? Those other rooms of torment whirled in front of my eyes; clean white rooms smelling of disinfectant, that dungeon of despair with the trash-littered yard outside a nailed-down window, and the high turret in mid-Manhattan from which I had attempted to leap. No matter what the room looked like here it could not help but be the stage as I went through the same painful processes.

First would come those days of pure, unadulterated hell. There would be those interminable hours which I counted off in faltering seconds, with their relentless sensations of intense anxiety and extreme nervousness. Unexpected sounds would make me jump awkwardly, as a mad marionette controlled by an idiot, and I would grit my teeth and bite parched lips to keep from screaming. Then I would.

After that would come the spasms in the stomach while my intestines growled and gurgled as they were starting to do now. Nausea would ram its iron fist against my abdomen, my heart pounding in such thunderous beats that the whole world must be able to hear it.

Through it all I'd sweat, as I was doing now while Harriet angled the car across the courtyard toward a circular driveway with a covered walk, all embraced by a towering building whose blank-faced windows frowned down on interlopers.

Next my nose would run and I'd yawn endlessly. Despite the perspiration, running in tumbling torrents, I'd have chills until my teeth would chatter. No matter how I'd strive to control them, my legs would jerk and I'd ache all over in bone-deep stabs. My flesh would quiver under a succession of hot flashes and icy chills.

Then it would get worse.

Monstrous figures from some ghastly nether region swarmed over my bed and leered down from the walls and ceiling. My screams ripped jagged holes in the night and I tore and smashed things, anything and everything, with the maniacal strength of agony and terror.

Through it all, from start to finish, every nerve in my body would thrash and burn, as they were doing now while Harriet swung the car to a standstill in front of a bank of steps leading to a pair of double doors.

"Coward, coward," I ranted inwardly. "If you hadn't been such a coward you wouldn't have let a little pain get you down."

Taking a tighter grip on myself I looked up at those waiting doors. What, I wondered, was behind them for me?

Not that it mattered too much. Those first few excrutiating days, already started, eventually would pass somehow. After that the nightmare would slack off and they'd soon have me back on my feet and once again I'd be "cured."

Those few days would save Harriet for me. That was the important thing. A couple of weeks here would straighten me out to the point where once again I could go home to her. Would it last this time? Who knew? The important thing was to restore the hope and the faith which Harriet had lost; to keep her beside me.

Then I realized that she had been sitting there watching me and I started guiltily, fearful that she might have been able to read my thoughts. Her knuckles stood out whitely as she gripped the steering wheel and her voice was low as she broke the silence.

"Well, Bill, we might as well go in."

Wearily, reluctantly, I nodded assent.

Drenched with nervous perspiration and heart hammering with renewed trepidation I clambered slowly from the car. Wordlessly I closed the car door behind me and climbed the steps mechanically until we stood at the top. I looked down at my hand on the doorknob as if it belonged to someone else and closed my eyes for an instant as all the old fears, doubts, and anxieties closed in around me.

"Oh, God," I groaned inwardly, "why has this happened to me? What has brought me here?"

Then I opened the door and we went inside.

It was the usual routine. Behind the reception desk sat an elderly woman who jotted down my name and then told us to take a seat in an adjoining waiting room with large glass windows. Through them I could see a tremendous sweep of green lawn having much the appearance of a public park.

"It looks like a nice place," Harriet observed.

I nodded but remained silent, busy fighting back the early qualms of drug withdrawal surging inside me. Nice place indeed, I thought. Blessed little of it I would see for the next few days, aside from a room in which I would go through hell clear from one side to the other. And for what? Considering the past, what could I expect from the future?

These dismal thoughts were interrupted by a voice behind us, calm, easy, and pleasant. "Mr. and Mrs. Stern?"

We turned from the windows and a tall young man in a tweed suit came up to us. He held out his hand, level eyes regarding us appraisingly through horn-rimmed glasses. "I am Dr. Gordon Edgren."

There was an easy friendliness about him, a compelling warmth which I felt instantly. But doctors were nothing new to me. I had seen hundreds of them. This, I thought fleetingly, was just another who would make me "well" for a few weeks, but unable to exorcize the demons or buttress the weakness which always before had forced me back to the needle, he had in the end no more chance than any other in that long, phantom line of white-coated men in my past.

Dr. Edgren talked briefly with us and then competently supervised my admission to the Institute. After this he took us to a section known as White Hall, a gray stone building of Old English architecture, where I climbed what seemed like innumerable stairs to reach my room on the second floor.

It was a bright, cheerful room, much as you would find in a better class hotel, with a comfortable double bed, a bureau, easy chair, floor lamp, and bright curtains at the window.

After I was settled Harriet bid me a restrained good-by which told me clearly that her feelings hadn't changed, and then left for the long drive back to Purchase. Dr. Edgren sat with me for a while and talked casually until I became accustomed to my surroundings. Finally, as he prepared to leave, he asked me, "Do you have any more medicine with you?"

"Yes," I confessed, and handed over the Demerol tablets which I had brought to this big, easy-going man who told me comfortingly that I would be given all the sleeping medicine

I needed that night and that someone would be with me constantly during the first few days.

"But our biggest problem," he warned, "is really the matter of sleeping medicine. Actually I don't regard the drugs as being half as menacing as the sleeping pills. You have never injected yourself, nor completely lost your sense of responsibility. It seems to me, from what you've told me, that the basic fault is the sleeping medicine. It's the crutch which inevitably has led you back to drugs."

It was, he told me, a matter of first things first, however, and our immediate consideration would be to get me off drugs.

Those next few days were every bit of the hell I expected from having gone through them so often before. I have described all of the horrible aches, pains, and delusions. This time, as result of my terrific drug buildup over the months since my release in January from Le Roy Hospital, it was more ghastly than ever.

From an addiction standpoint, never had I been in such sorrowful shape. This time the withdrawal was worse than it ever had been, with almost unendurable pain that it seemed would never cease. The gallery of ghouls, gibbering insanely, was larger than ever, and I would have destroyed myself if I could have found some means of doing so.

Dr. Edgren was at my side when I needed him most, yet standing firm against my craven, frenzied pleading for just one merciful injection.

"This will pass," he soothed me, over and over again until, when I was alone, I chanted it to myself.

I sneered at him and cursed him, meanwhile raving constantly during that first agonizing week before the nightmare began to subside. But then, as he said, it did begin to pass.

Through it all I felt always the tragic uselessness of this

terrible battle. I had been through this so often before. Certainly it would pass. I would go home. And then some day, God only knew when, I'd go through it again and again and again until finally I would run out of tomorrows.

It was, I shuddered in resigned exhaustion, merely the same old meaningless mummery. I was on a carousel of calamity which I seemed destined to ride into eternity.

Chapter 17

I have lost the immortal
part of myself, and what
remains is bestial.
—Shakespeare

EVER SO GRADUALLY, infinitesimally, the worst of the drug withdrawal symptoms subsided and yet I was still so tense and nervous that I couldn't sleep. While I was drying out on the drugs Dr. Edgren permitted me the support of the sleeping medicine of which, as mentioned, I was taking as many as sixteen tablets a night.

Throughout the drug withdrawal at White Hall, even with the aid of sleeping pills I could obtain no rest. Even when the worst of the craving subsided, I still paced the floor endlessly throughout the nights. After another week, in which each succeeding night was as sleepless as the last, one of the nurses showed great concern. "You know Mr. Stern," she shook her head, "we never have had a patient here who does as little sleeping as you do."

Even so, Dr. Edgren very slowly began to cut down on the sleeping medicine. At first I was reduced to twelve tablets, then to ten, and finally one evening Dr. Edgren came into my room and asked me if I thought I could get by with eight.

"We have been trying to knock down this sleeping medicine intake little by little," he informed me. "Now, don't you think you could get by with eight, Bill?"

"Yes," I told him, not knowing how it would be possible but feeling that it was all I could say. "I guess I can."

For several days I received eight pills and then I began to feel as if even the eight weren't doing as much for me as they had before. There was just one answer.

Carefully, when my eight pills were brought to me that evening, I cut them to pieces. It was as I had expected. Four of them were decoys, nothing but sugar-coated pills masked in the same outer substance as the sleeping tablets.

I was enraged. Did they think they were dealing with a child? Imagine trying to trick me in such a silly manner! Furiously I rang for the nurse, and when she appeared I really raked her over the coals. She stood there, startled and wide-eyed, as I fumed and cursed at her, Dr. Edgren, and the Institute.

"I'm a voluntary patient, not a charity case," I roared, livid and shaking. "I'm supposed to have eight of these, damn it, so you'd better be damned sure to bring me eight."

Within a couple of days, however, it was the same thing all over again. Painstaking dissection of the pills showed me that once more half of them were imitations. And, in my insecure mental condition, I slyly determined to "get even." If they wanted to act this way Bill Stern could play the same game. Let them go their deceptive way and I'd go mine.

Thus, when Dr. Edgren summoned me to his office for the first of what were to be daily psychiatric sessions designed to get at the cause of my troubles and obliterate them, some inner perversity made me decide to balk his every move. Of course it wasn't an intelligent reaction. But in my unbalanced physical state and uncertain mental condition I had developed the animal-like feelings of someone who was being trapped and persecuted.

In Dr. Edgren's quiet, comfortable office, with its pleasant walls of light green and its soft flowered draperies, I had a completely relaxed feeling. And yet I couldn't get it through the devious pattern of my thinking that this friendly man, puffing serenely on his pipe, was vitally interested in helping me. Why should he be? No other doctor ever had been.

Easily, effortlessly, he probed into my past with questions which held no offense. Despite this receptive attitude and his dedicated kindliness I felt as though I were some kind of a curious bug under a scientist's microscope. The answers I gave him were highly colored, reflecting only the best of Bill Stern.

The truth of it, as I look back on that early period, is that because of the bitter realism of the past I expected no permanent good to result from any of this. A few weeks and Harriet would come for me. I would sign myself out, as a voluntary patient has a right to do, and I would return home. This was my fight, nobody else's, so why should I bare my innermost thoughts and feelings to this stranger? Why should he, in some future years when he lectured classes in psychology, tell his students about the personal psychological problems of Bill Stern?

Inspecting those days in my memory I am convinced that I wasn't getting any better, aside from having, momentarily, conquered the drug habit. Conquered it? Even that I didn't know with certainty. After all, I had "conquered" it before only to fall back into the same dreadful pattern at the first sign of adversity.

I was making little, if any, headway toward complete and actual recovery. I was quieter, yes, and more docile and generally easier to handle. But I continued to fight against the complete withdrawal of sleeping medicine although they tried every device they knew.

Nor did I make it easier for them. Restless and bored with the same room after about a month, and always in the back of my mind expecting to leave the Institute at the first sign from Harriet that she thought I might be well enough to return home, I played fully the role of the famous Bill Stern.

I was the man who always traveled first-class. I demanded a suite of rooms. I bullied the nurses, sending them scurrying for ice water, towels, or anything else I could think of. These tactics swiftly alienated all those around me, but rather than making me treat them more considerately their rejection made me just that much more irritable, and in the end more intent on aggravating them.

Dr. Edgren was aware from the first of my self-imposed isolation. He suggested that, in what is an integral part of the therapy at the Institute, I should participate in the general program for all patients. This included such varied and diverting activities as the bridge club, shopwork, discussion sessions, dancing, and staging plays.

"I get paid for entertaining," I told him curtly. "As for bridge and that other nonsense, who needs it?"

He didn't press me. A man of deep perception, Dr. Edgren knew from the first that he wasn't getting through to me. No matter how hard he tried or what he did, there was no rapport between us. I wasn't yet ready for harmony, accord, or any association with others. Also, as he painstakingly labored over his notes of our interviews, for which I concocted fanciful and highly-embroidered tales of the Bill Stern I had wanted to be and wished him to see, even his infinite patience was strained.

"Bill," he finally remonstrated with me during one of our sessions in the solitude of his office, "it's come down to a question between us of who is going to be the boss."

Angrily I started to interrupt but he held up a restraining hand and continued. "Let's face facts, Bill. You're being resistive and you must stop it if we are ever going to do you any good."

Hotly I denied this. He listened quietly, letting me finish my rambling dissertation. Then he looked at me steadily and there was no compromise in his tone as he gave it to me straight from the shoulder.

"Look, Bill, frankly I don't believe you had any valid intention of going off drugs."

Wide-eyed, I stared at him as he paused, his eyes never wavering from mine. Then his low, level voice resumed, damning me in its certainty, as he added, "It is my honest opinion that you came here only because of the threat of losing your wife and your job."

There was no answer I could think of; no excuse I could find ready at the tip of my usually glib tongue. This man read me as easily as he would a book of children's nursery rhymes.

Still I wasn't ready to concede.

That night, in my defensive anger and self-pity, as well as my hidden shame at the picture he had drawn of me with those few words, I was more irritable than ever. Did this man think I was a lunatic? Irascibly I snapped at the nurses, demanding more sleeping medicine, and when they wouldn't give it to me without an order from Dr. Edgren I flew into a tantrum. When this had no effect I cried out that I was having terrible pains in my leg. Dr. Edgren was summoned, and while he talked to me soothingly he gave me no further medication.

July and August crept past on leaden feet and my only dream now was to get Harriet to consent to my release so that I could return home. Then, in early September, as the football season was about to commence, I became even more emotionally disturbed when I read a story in *Variety* which made me feel that my career was beyond recall.

It was only a small box of type and yet it might as well have been edged in mourning black. I read it, over and over, the one-line "head" scourging my very soul.

September 5, 1956

SPORTSCASTER TOLL

On a somewhat more somber note, the new TV-radio season will be minus the services of three of the all-time standout sports announcers, all of whom are gravely ill.

They are Bill Stern, who is presently in a sanitarium; Ted Husing and Bill Slater. Latter two have been in poor health for some time.

Fourth among the all-timers is, of course, Graham McNamee, who died some years back.

What an ending, I thought disconsolately, crumpling the paper into a ball and hurling it into a corner, only to pick it up, smooth it out, read it again, and then throw it violently away from me once more.

I was further disturbed when, while taking a walk through the grounds, I met Gene Tierney. I was strolling along the flower-bordered path, not noticing anything in particular but immersed in my own gloomy thoughts, when she approached and introduced herself. We chatted briefly about mutual friends and acquaintances and then she went on her way.

This beautiful, dark-haired woman already was one of

Hollywood's great stars when she appeared on my Colgate show in 1944. In those days she had been vivacious and apparently serene. Now, while she still was impeccably groomed, there was a tragic sadness about her. A deep melancholy settled over me as I watched her walk away. What prank of fate had caused each of us to wind up here in such grievous extremity?

Bitterness and despair took an even tighter grasp on me after this and shortly thereafter, on September 12, 1956, came the crushing clmax to which I had been building through all of these terrible years.

On that day I had an exceptionally severe kidney stone attack; a real one, not of the imagined variety. And, as fate would have it, Dr. Edgren was away from the Institute when it occurred.

In view of my previous attitude and medical history, further marred by lack of co-operation and determined unresponsiveness, there was immediate suspicion that this attack was not a legitimate one. The doctor who attended me in Dr. Edgren's absence ordered tests, however, and they disclosed that a kidney stone actually was present.

The resultant treatment was a mistake. I was given an injection of morphine to ease the pain.

It was a needle prick which aroused all of those lightly sleeping demons within my body.

After this I was taken to the nearby Hartford Hospital where I could be hospitalized in the fullest sense of the word until after I passed the stone.

There, more morphine was administered.

Being back in the septic, impersonal confines of a hospital with all the familiar odors I knew so well, in addition to the heady sensations of the morphine for which in my insatiable hunger I had yearned so long and achingly, immediately rekindled my craving to an unprecedented fever pitch. It was like touching flame to a powder keg.

My awakened voracity knew no bounds; drugs I had to have or, I thought, I would go completely out of my mind. Desire racked me even after I had passed the stone and in a frenzy I summoned the nurse.

She absolutely refused to give me an injection. "We have been given strict orders against it," she told me. "What you had was necessary; but no more."

It was more than I could endure. I screamed and I cursed, ripping up my bed covering and becoming so wild and disorderly that on the second day they moved me unceremoniously from my regular room to the psychopathic ward.

Even here, desire raging within me and my body on fire, I continued my incessant and insistent clamor, ringing the bell frenziedly for the nurses, shouting obscenities, and prayerfully pleading for drugs. Rather than getting better or becoming resigned to the fact that they weren't going to give me any more drugs I became increasingly worse as the hours of denial passed.

Unable to quiet me, the doctors at Hartford Hospital on the third day finally telephoned Dr. Edgren. They told him that they were unable to handle me and that the Institute would have to come and take me away immediately.

Within the hour the door to my room opened and four attendants from the Institute entered to take me back. I was having none of it or them; nothing would do for me except an injection of morphine. At first they attempted to reason with me, but I would not be hushed or mollified.

Soon they saw that there was no recourse except to assist me, but when one of them took my arm I reared back insanely and smashed a fist into his face. There was nothing left for them to do but to restrain me forcibly, which they did, yet even so I broke away from them once we were outside and tried to escape into the night.

The nightmare journey back to the Institute finally was completed, and because I was so violent and unmanageable Dr. Edgren ordered an injection of Pentothal Sodium to knock me out.

My awakening was a shattering shock.

I was in the sickest ward, a locked unit for disturbed psychotics, penned in with others who, through the strange vagaries of the human mind, are bent on self-destruction or are dangerous to others.

The stark realization of my rock-bottom predicament came slowly as I opened my eyes to a small, cell-like room barely eight feet long by six feet wide. I was lying on a single bed with my artificial leg beside me, and struggling to sit up I saw that the only other piece of furniture in this carpetless cell of confinement was a heavy bureau. A thick, unbreakable screen shrouded the one window and there was a light set far up in the unusually high ceiling. Another light was set into the wall, above the baseboard behind a glass panel. This light, I was to discover, was left on at night so that the attendants could maintain a continuous watch on the patient through an eight-inch square porthole of unbreakable glass in the sturdy door.

A scream began to build up in my throat, tearing its way past my clenched teeth. The sound ripped through the tiny room, keening off the walls in a rising reverberation of terror. Almost instantly the door opened and two attendants entered the room and tried to pacify me.

"Please try to get hold of yourself, Mr. Stern," one of them said soothingly as he walked toward the bed.

Grabbing my artificial leg I lashed out at him. Throwing

up one arm to ward off my blows, he backed quickly away and then, standing in the doorway, told me, "You have behaved very badly. Dr. Edgren has ordered that from now on you are to be kept under the strictest regulations."

"Get the hell out of here," I raved. "Get out and tell Edgren that I want him."

Dr. Edgren wasn't long in arriving and my anger bubbled over again when I saw him. Fluidly I cursed him, and after listening to me a few minutes he advised me calmly, "Bill, the time has come when you're going to have to cut the mustard by yourself. We can watch every move you make in here. As long as you are our patient we must have the control and there isn't anything you can do about it."

I was building up to another verbal explosion as he added, "Not only that, but from now on you don't get a single bit of sleeping medicine."

Snatching up my artificial leg I hurled it at him. The leg struck against the wall beside him, scant inches from his head, and clattered to the floor. Dr. Edgren stooped slowly and picked it up.

"I'll just take this with me until you need it again," was all he said. Then he left.

For a few minutes I lay there silently, sunk in utter frustration. Then a blazing fury began to boil through me anew. They weren't going to keep Bill Stern locked up like an idiot. Sliding off the bed, I hopped to the door, intending to smash it open with my head if necessary. One last violent plunge sent me slamming into the door, and to my complete surprise I discovered that it wasn't locked. The door flew open as I crashed into it and I tumbled on through into the corridor beyond, falling flat on my face and lying there in a sobbing heap.

The corridor opened up into a larger room with a number

of beds and two attendants hurried to me from there. Gently but firmly they carried me, crying and protesting, back into my tiny room. Placing me on the bed they left, and I lay there panting, heaving, and all the time scheming.

All right, if they wouldn't let me out I'd do away with myself. But what could I use? My eyes fell on the glass panel covering the night light low on the wall. Rolling off the bed I hammered on the panel with my fists, determined to break it and get a piece of glass with which to slash my wrists and end this ignominious misery. Yet even here I was thwarted. The glass was unbreakable, designed to defy just such intentions as mine, and I finally collapsed beside it in a heap of frustration.

Throughout the next day and night I wore myself down with that terrible craving, hurling myself again and again through the doorway, screaming and cursing at the attendants, refusing to eat, having to be forced to go to the bathroom, tearing up my bedclothes, and striking out at anyone and everyone who came within reach.

Even Dr. Edgren's seemingly unlimited patience finally began to wear thin, and after one particularly violent episode in which I savagely struck an attendant he was visibly upset. His voice was troubled as he came into my room.

"What is it now?" he asked.

"The attendants have been beating me," I lied without a qualm. "They've beaten me black and blue."

"Take off your pajamas and show me," he ordered.

Hesitantly I disrobed and stood naked before him.

"Well," Dr. Edgren said wearily, "just where are the marks of this terrible beating?"

"They must be there," I shouted, straining to look over my shoulder at my back. "Don't you see them?"

"No," he answered, "and the reason is simply because nobody has laid a finger on you."

"You're a liar," I screamed.

Passionately I accused everybody, him included, of trying to hurt me. Then he hushed me, his voice filled with resignation.

"Bill," he said sorrowfully, "there isn't a thing we can do for you if you won't help us."

"All I want is to get out of here," I snapped back, my voice strident.

Dr. Edgren shook his head in patent discouragement. "Well," he admitted, "you signed yourself in voluntarily. If you insist on it, you also can sign yourself out."

With a resigned shrug he turned his back and without another word walked out of my room.

No sooner had he gone than I yelled for an attendant and roughly demanded a pencil and paper. They were damned well right, I thought. I would sign myself out. Who did they think they were, keeping me, Bill Stern, behind locked doors? I was here of my own volition and they had absolutely no right to do this. Thus did I bluster to myself as I waited for the writing materials.

The attendant brought them to me within a few minutes, and standing on one leg in front of the bureau slowly and laboriously I began to write the letter demanding my release. It was a struggle. Forming the words, or trying to, was an astonishingly laborious process. But finally I finished it, amazed at the difficulty I had had in accomplishing such a simple task, and I brusquely told the attendant to see that it was delivered to the doctor at once.

It was the next day before Dr. Edgren returned. When he walked in he had my letter in his hand.

"Bill," he tried to reason with me, "you don't want to do

this. If you leave now you'll never have a chance to get yourself completely well."

I was imperious and curt. "I want out. That's all I want from you and what happens to me is nobody's business but my own."

Dr. Edgren said no more and I assumed that the issue was settled.

But what I didn't know was that he already was preparing to act. After realizing that he could not reason with me enough to talk me into staying voluntarily, he had telephoned Harriet as a desperate last resort and told her in full detail what had been happening and how I was acting. He advised her to start commitment proceedings.

When I heard of this I went into another violent rage and then, gradually, anger was replaced by terror.

Harriet, who always had stood faithfully beside me, wouldn't let me down. Or would she, in view of her attitude when I came here and this latest series of events? I wasn't certain, but soon that question was answered for me with dreadful finality.

Harriet came to the Institute, as I sat with her and the doctor she asked him, "If he is allowed to leave, will he go back to drugs?"

Dr. Edgren's reply consisted of one word, crisp, authoritative, and final, "Unquestionably."

That one word settled the issue. Harriet, instead of bowing to my will, agreed with the doctor and they prepared to have me committed.

Under this type of proceeding a person judged incapable becomes a ward of the state and can no longer sign himself out. As required by law I would be examined by two disinterested psychiatrists who were not connected with the Institute. It would be their duty to decide whether I was in full possession of my faculties or whether I should be legally committed.

Ultimately I was taken before the first of these psychiatrists, and from his reactions and the manner in which he eyed me I realized with a sinking heart that it had gone badly, so badly that I demanded to be allowed to see an attorney. Dr. Edgren consented and I was permitted to telephone my lawyer in New York in a frantic effort to keep from being committed.

It was a word, commitment, which terrified me. I was certain that if I were committed I would have to spend the rest of my life behind those locked doors at the Institute, imprisoned without recourse behind those baleful portholes, buried forever from the world.

The lawyer advised me that he would be present at the commitment hearing to make certain that everything was being handled legally, but from the manner in which he said it I knew my case was hopeless.

The second and final commitment examination was scheduled for a Saturday afternoon. I waited behind the locked doors of the large ward in the disturbed unit, fretting on the edge of my chair and entirely unconscious of those other poor souls about me.

High in the wall at one end of the room, far out of reach of the disturbed patients with whom I was grouped, was a television set. Vaguely I became conscious that one of the attendants had switched on the set, and struggling to focus my attention on it I saw that a football game was being telecast.

Vaguely I heard that this was the opening game of the season. Chin sunk on chest, I tried to figure out how many years it had been since I had missed broadcasting an opening game. The mathematics troubled me. Let's see, now I began in 1934 and this was 1956. Was it twenty-two years? My puzzled concentration was broken as an attendant stopped beside me and cheerfully attempted to engage me in conversation.

"This will be a good game, Mr. Stern," he said with that fan enthusiasm I had known so well in the past.

Wordlessly, I nodded.

"I guess you've seen so many of them that it's hard for you to work up much interest," he added.

No answer came from me as I peered unseeingly into nowhere, sinking more deeply into my depressing thoughts.

Not interested? I'd give anything to be out there in that booth right this minute, back as a part of that gripping excitement, clutching the microphone in my eager hand, and living a life which I had never actually appreciated until this miserable moment. And here I sat, locked in the disturbed unit of a mental hospital, and about to be committed to a life behind locks, possibly forever.

I slumped back into the chair and the tears rolled down my cheeks.

Bitterly, hopelessly, I knew the taste of ashes.

Chapter 18

Deceive not thy physician.
—George Herbert

IT WAS AT THIS LOWEST of all ebb tides in my life, broken in heart and spirit as well as in health, that Dr. Edgren through some great intuitive sense decided to make one last effort to save me from myself.

He knew, with infinite wisdom, that these commitment proceedings were doing me more harm than even a sane and sound man could endure. No matter what the cost, he was determined not to allow me to surrender to my weaknesses and appetites and go on to the inevitable destruction which assuredly awaited me.

Even at this eleventh hour he would not resign himself to the almost indisputable fact that I wouldn't fight for myself. So as I sat there, crushed and beaten, in the disturbed ward during my disconsolate wait for the final commitment hearing, he came into the room and sat down beside me.

Leaning back with a sigh he crossed his long legs and lighted his pipe. Then he began to talk, slowly, almost coaxingly, and with gentle understanding; the sounds of the football telecast forming a mocking backdrop.

"You know, Bill," he said, "it isn't too late to help yourself. These whole proceedings aren't necessary and don't have to be carried through if you'll just admit that you need help and will try to help yourself and give me your co-operation."

Cautious against some trick, I waited wordlessly.

Dr. Edgren didn't hurry. He tamped his pipe and relighted it. Then he continued. "All you would have to do is to withdraw your letter of intent to leave. You must know that your wife loves you and wants nothing except that you get better. Remember, this is just as hard on her as it is on you. Certainly you don't believe that she wants to hurt you. Now do you?"

I shook my head. No, Harriet didn't want anything but the best for us. That I knew. How long and desperately had she tried? And how could she have stood it all these years? I was, quite suddenly and unexpectedly, seeing her side of this nightmare, seeing it vividly as it must have been for her in all this time of torment.

"But you must withdraw that letter and you must make up your mind to stay here peacefully, helping us to get at the root of all your troubles," Dr. Edgren added. "We all know that it won't be easy; no more tantrums, no more lies, no more medicine. But, Bill, it's the only true way out of this thing. Actually, it's all in your hands. No matter what I do, or what anyone else does, the final answer is with you alone."

Pausing, giving me time to assimilate what he had said, Dr. Edgren continued. "If you do it my way," he promised, "we can halt these commitment proceedings right now. You'll still be a voluntary patient even though we know among ourselves that you still have to earn that position and there will be many difficult steps ahead."

It was a reprieve, the thought leaped into my mind. I felt as a man unexpectedly pardoned from the gallows. And I looked at Dr. Edgren with vast new respect. For the first time I had found someone with a will stronger than my own; someone more determined that I was going to get well than I was that I must remain a victim of myself and my own weaknesses.

It was a startling revelation to me that this man, who had been through the distress and trouble which I had caused, still had the faith and willingness to help me. It was as if a blind man was seeing for the first time as, in one perceptive instant, it suddenly seemed so right and so easy to place myself with complete trust and confidence in the hands of this kind, understanding man. I wondered inanely why it hadn't occurred to me before.

With tears dimming my vision, I thrust out my hand and grasped his. "I'll withdraw the letter," I wept. "I'll withdraw it and I swear I'll put myself entirely in your hands, Doctor. Whatever you say, I promise you, that will be it."

It was at this moment God willed I should get well.

Not that it came all at once, as with the simple turning on of a light. For after years and years of constant regression and this latest mad craving which had torn loose inside of me since my trip to the hospital, freeing my ravening appetite for drugs once again, I was within a shade of being a broken man in flesh and mind. The commitment worries had been the capping climax and never had I been more nerve-racked, underweight, and generally run-down. But, irrevocably, even I knew now that it was all or nothing.

There was to be, for several days, a period in which the old unbridled anger rode me savagely, a panting wrestling with those unleashed appetites for drugs, morbid sessions of extreme depression in which I wondered bitterly whether it was all worth-while, nervous crying spells, and an inability to eat or rest.

Dr. Edgren at first considered giving me shock treatments but decided instead on hydrotherapy baths to relieve my tensions and anxieties. Then, while I lay in the sheet-covered tub, the warm waters soothing my nerves and easing my tired, aching flesh, the Doctor's steady voice provided added comfort.

Over and over again I strengthened my will by telling myself that only my complete co-operation and willingness to help him in his efforts to help me could provide the total answer. Too, the nearness of those commitment proceedings was a ready spur to my determination.

For the first time, far back in the deepest recesses of my mind, I began to think and honestly believe that I really could get well.

Discarded, thanks to Dr. Edgren's support, were my ideas of merely passing the time in the Institute until I could sign myself out. Now I strove to be helpful, to try to assist the Doctor in every way possible.

The violence within me vanished as though it had been a puff of smoke. The change in me was almost unbelievable. I began to eat, and drained by the hydrotherapy baths, for the first time in years knew the refreshing wonder of undrugged sleep. Much of this was due, too, to the use of tranquilizers, which Dr. Edgren informed me were non-narcotic and non-habit forming.

It seemed almost unbelievable, when after only ten days I was taken out of the disturbed ward and moved into an eight-bed unit where there were few restrictions.

I was almost too excited and happy for words when Dr.

Edgren told me that I was being moved. In the disturbed ward I felt less than a man, for in there one was not allowed to light a match or smoke a cigarette unless it was lighted for him, nor permitted to have ties, belts, or bathrobe cords for fear that he might somehow do away with himself.

And always, a silent torment in the back of your mind, there were those locks on the doors.

"You've earned this transfer, Bill," Dr. Edgren smiled. "You have an absolutely amazing constitution, with phenomenal recuperative powers, and neither mentally nor physically do you belong in here any longer."

All I could do was grin and shake his hand gratefully.

"And, Bill," he added, "you might like to know that your progress is almost unheard of here. In the last couple of years only one other person that I know of has made such a rapid jump from the disturbed unit to an open unit."

My new quarters weren't more than forty yards from the disturbed unit, up a short flight of stairs and through a door into another section of the building.

But they were on the other side of the lock.

The mere knowledge that the doors were open, that I was not under lock and key, was an inspiring experience. There was suddenly a new buoyancy within me, a light-heartedness I had not known in years.

Now, too, the hydrotherapy baths were supplanted by the non-habit forming tranquilizers which Dr. Edgren continued for a brief time longer in order to keep the tensions from returning. We also went back to the comfortable privacy of his sound-proofed office for our daily psychiatric sessions.

This time there was no nonsense. There was no attempt on my part to tell him exaggerated stories of the dashing Bill Stern I earlier had insisted that he see. There was absolutely no restraint left within me, for I understood at last, completely and thoroughly, that this man was interested in me as a friend and would do everything in his power to help me.

This time it was a relief to discuss all of the annoyances and problems which I had stored up behind the dam of my mind throughout the driving years of misery. At times I talked, it seemed, for hours without interruption. At other times, when I couldn't seem to get my thoughts free, Dr. Edgren would sit patiently at ease, puffing his pipe in silence. Then the dam would break again and the words gush forth.

I told him everything. Of my boyhood during which Father had stood between me and deserved retribution whenever I was in a jam; my feeling that Mother was too stern; the lack of warmth at home; the need to belong to someone; and my failure to become the great athlete I had visions of being.

Of the prejudice I felt in my teens because I was Jewish and how later, whenever I was rejected for an assignment or by a sponsor, I always attributed it to this prejudice.

Of the terrible disillusion and pain when I lost my leg and the anguish of body and mind which through the years had sent me scurrying for the solace of the needle.

Of the excessive pride in the success I had won despite all of these obstacles; of the merciless feeling that I must always win at everything I attempted.

And of the beaten feeling which came over me finally that I could never defeat the drugs.

Patiently and sympathetically he listened, questioning and probing every detail of my life. I found that it was a great relief to bare my heart, almost as though I were shifting the burden of my guilt, terror, and anxiety to his shoulders. Brought out into the open, after years of being hidden in the depths of my mind, they didn't seem as frightful or frightening as they had when they were buried within me.

Once the long hours of listening were over, Dr. Edgren little by little analyzed and explained these once unbearable fears, driving home the long-avoided knowledge that life and its intricacies must be accepted as they are, without illusion or delusion.

Volumes would be required to tell of the hours, the days, and the weeks of discussion, counter-discussion, and finally the revelation which was mine in that tiny chamber of comfort. But the sum and substance of it is imprinted indelibly on my mind.

I have only to close my eyes and again I can see Dr. Edgren as he said, "Let's look at your boyhood, Bill. Your father was a compulsive businessman, driven by his own inner spur to the supreme interest of making money. You can't say this was a terrible fault and yet it left him too little time to spend with you. The compensating factor in his own mind, without doubt, was to give you too many material things, and whenever you were in trouble to come through with the money to bail you out. It was only natural, as a boy, that you unconsciously would get yourself into difficulties so that he would come to your aid. In this way you managed to obtain from him the attention you wanted.

"On the other hand," he added, "your mother, knowing that right was right and being a person who could tolerate no wrong, was rigid and disapproving of such developments. This created within you a rejection of your mother because such an attitude stood in your way to obtaining attention from your father. Therefore, without realizing it, you were manipulating your parents for your own gain and to obtain the feeling, which you needed so desperately, that someone loved you. All of this was compounded, Bill, by your athletic failures and the feeling you never 'belonged,' anywhere or to anyone."

The willful pattern of my boyhood, extending on into my aggressive manhood, became clear to me. Each struggle, each frustration, had led to another. But Dr. Edgren made it obvious to me without any element of shame being involved; it was simply cause and effect of an unsteady foundation on which it had been impossible to build a serene and successful life.

This baring of one fear uncovered the seat of the others. I had ever been particularly sensitive to racial prejudice, real or imagined, believing firmly that many of my failures, socially or in business, were due to the fact that certain bigoted people rejected me.

"There are certain people who nurse these prejudices," Dr. Edgren confirmed. "Certainly there can be no question of that. But, Bill," he explained, "there are always those who hold prejudices against any race or creed but their own. This has ever been the way of the world and who is to say that it will ever change.

"The best thing to do, when you are involved with people such as these, is to ignore them. Don't let it get under your skin, for they are the ones who need pity. You must hold your tongue, turn your other cheek, and pray for them.

"The fact is," he added, "that you have dwelt too much on this and built it up out of all proportion. And it is traceable, this feeling that you are not accepted for such a reason, to your own basic inadequacy. Always there has been a question in your mind of not being accepted; by your father and then, in your teens and later years, by certain elements of society. Again you felt rejected. It raised within you a doubt as to whether anyone loved you, with the resultant surmise that if they didn't there must be something wrong with you, personally."

Had he used a scalpel Dr. Edgren could not have laid the

inside of me more widely open for analytical inspection. Working as a master surgeon, yet withal in a kindly and understanding way, he dragged all of those long-hidden fears out into the open and killed them off in the antiseptic sunlight of truth and understanding.

"Let's look at the pain which has been the basic excuse for your desire to take drugs," he pointed out. "It was just that, an excuse, strengthened by all these other buried fears. Because much of your pain is psychogenic or, in plain words, simply imaginary.

"Why is this? That's easily understood, Bill, if you will stop and think. Underneath everything else you have a terrible fear of failure. You've been at the top of the heap for a long time and unconsciously you keep thinking that there's no place else for you to go but down. This accounts for the feeling that you must win and win eternally and the thought frightens you. It shouldn't. You've had extraordinary success and there is no reason in the world why you can't go on always having your full share of it. Certainly there will be ups and downs, because no one wins forever. But you will always have your share if you'll let your courage equal your talent.

"Then, too," he explained, patiently probing ever deeper, "having lost your leg made you feel inadequate, and you continually tried to compensate for the feeling that you weren't a whole person. But remember, Bill, the leg was gone when a fine woman decided that she still wanted and needed you as a husband. And your greatest success came after you had lost that leg.

"Still you medicated yourself so that, in the recesses of your mind, you felt that you were able to function. But let's face it, your success both in love and business proved that such actions were unnecessary.

"And, Bill," he concluded, "you have to face up to the fact that one afflicted with such leg and kidney stone troubles has no other course but to learn to live with pain. The real pains you will be able to endure if the psychogenic ones are eliminated. And they can be if you will only learn to understand yourself and think more of those who depend on you than you do of your own harbored woes and ailments."

There was much, much more in those talks, which gave me the first real and unvarnished introduction to myself I had ever had. I knew, with brilliant clarity, the truth and value of Dr. Edgren's suggestion to "stop playing a role and simply be yourself."

I had been, I thought in surprise, a man who cravenly refused to face life, and in so doing had come perilously close to losing it.

Bill Stern, the actor, died in that warm, comfortable little office. Bill Stern, the man, was born.

Happily, as the weeks went by, I felt a tremendous difference in my association with others. In the eight-bed unit to which I was moved I began for the first time to take an interest in my companions. It was a strange and yet a remarkably satisfying feeling, which produced a wonderful inner glow, not to be "on stage" at all times, to be relieved of the necessity of being a constant performer who had to be the perennial center of attraction.

How long had it been, I wondered, since I had really listened to the conversation of others; their stories of the past, their hopes of the future, their dreams, disappointments, and frustrations? Everyone has his troubles; it dawned on me as if I actually had discovered some new scientific marvel, but only the weak and the unwilling bow down before them and permit themselves to be drowned in their own miseries.

My appetite was good, I slept well, and there was a new joy

in breathing the fresh air and seeing the blueness of the sky, as my attitude and outlook slowly but surely altered.

Eagerly now I anticipated Harriet's visits. Only now, for the first time in years, it was she who did the talking. In this rejuvenation of mine I listened with eager enjoyment as she told me of the doings at home, the antics of the children, the gossip of the neighborhood, and the friskiness of our French poodles. Now, suddenly, these were the things which were important.

When she was not with me I threw myself wholeheartedly into the daily program at the Institute. No longer driven by a relentless need to be the eternal hub of attention or a determination to win at everything, I was amazed to discover the enjoyment and relaxation of simple pastimes such as the once-scorned game of bridge. The sad plight of some of the other poor souls in the Institute began to plague me and I worked more feverishly than I ever had in the early days at the Music Hall to put on a play for the patients.

Life was becoming righter and brighter every day and it was with genuine distress that I overheard two of the patients in my unit bitterly discussing plans to leave the Institute because they didn't feel that they were making any progress. I spent hours with them, pleading and working my amateur psychology, unashamedly describing in minute detail the fears and problems which I had surmounted. It was a great thrill, a personal triumph to compare with any in my career, when both of them finally told me that they had taken new heart and decided to remain and fight it out "just as you have."

One of them, without my knowing it, went so far as to inform Dr. Edgren that it was I who had changed their minds.

"They told me what you did for them, Bill," he said

softly so that the others wouldn't hear. "It's the best sign of all. I know now that you're really fighting and will keep on fighting because you understand yourself. I want you to know," he added before saying good-night, "that I'm proud of you."

I felt as though I had won the Medal of Honor. I was so exuberantly delighted that as the lights were extinguished I knew that I wouldn't be able to sleep. The next thing I knew it was morning.

On December 22, 1956, six months after I had entered the Institute Of Living, three months and ten days after I had my last kidney stone attack and was removed to Hartford Hospital, three months and one week after I had been committed to the Institute's disturbed unit, and two months and twenty-seven days after being moved to my eight-bed unrestrained unit, I was summoned to Dr. Edgren's office.

As I walked in, Harriet, looking more beautiful than ever and with a radiant smile on her face, arose from one of those red leather chairs which I had used so long, so often, and to such good effect.

Throwing her arms around my neck while Dr. Edgren smiled delightedly over his pipe, Harriet hugged me joyously. "Bill," she said, "let's go home!"

Chapter 19

Resolve to be thyself: and know, that he
Who finds himself, loses his misery.
—Matthew Arnold

THERE IS NO EXPLAINING, if I used millions of words, the joy of my home-coming.

It was a cold, blustery day in late December, 1956. The trees were bare of leaves, the sky a dull, overcast gray, and the sweep of our lawn appeared much like a tattered, moth-eaten brown carpet left to fall into dust in an ancient attic.

Yet to me, as Harriet drove up our winding driveway, it was the most beautiful sight I had ever seen. Even after we stopped and Harriet switched off the engine, I simply sat there, my eyes devouring every detail, each bit of shrubbery and each familiar but almost forgotten particular.

Home again!

It surged through me with a giddy headiness. Nothing would do but that, before going inside, I should walk completely around the house. Much as a child nursing an ice cream cone, I was saving the inside for last.

Then, unable to wait longer, I crossed the threshold, and with Harriet's hand in mine toured each of the rooms with the reverent awe of a pilgrim visiting a shrine. Never before, it seemed, had I noticed how tastefully and beautifully this wife of mine had furnished and decorated our home, nor appreciated how comfortable and cozy it was.

I was home.

Two lazy and wonderful weeks slipped past and I felt complete, filled with a surging vitality. My convalescence was almost four months old by this time and the urge was growing ever stronger to return to my work.

I was home and yet, as soon I discovered, I was a long way from being back as far as my career was concerned.

My first course was to make a trip to the city to see if there was anything available. After six months in limbo I expected it to be difficult, and as I drove to New York I was filled with trepidation; concerned about my future, if I even had one, and not too certain that, after the debacle at New Orleans and the succeeding months of misery and steadily worsening personal performances, anyone would want to give me a job or trust me again. It would, I knew, be tough.

It was twice as tough as I expected it to be.

Nothing is deader than yesterday's newspaper or, it might be added, last year's broadcaster; particularly a voice which whispers in the trade insinuated had gone irrevocably bad. Old friends were pleasant, but evasive. New faces were friendly, but noncommital. As one disappointing day led to another it appeared that there might be no jobs forthcoming for Bill Stern.

Growing ever stronger within me was the feeling that

wherever I went, the memories of my past were too raw and livid for me ever to get another chance.

Each rejection was a stinging slap on the face and yet, despite the growing fear that I was the victim of a general boycott, I felt a strange jubilation at my reaction to the receptions.

Indicative of the change in Bill Stern, this time I didn't blame anyone else, nor rant and rave at those who previously would have been the targets of my hostility. I was discouraged, naturally. But now I could understand their side of it, too. There was no thought of going off the deep end as I would have done in the past. Now, I realized with a new found perception, I had to bide my time, wait for my chance, and then prove to a doubting world that Bill Stern wasn't merely as good as before but that he was better.

No longer were there fears of my ability. In the solitude of my basement playroom I made tape recordings which proved to me that my voice had recaptured all of its former timbre and depth. Eating with an almost unknown gusto and sleeping more peacefully than I ever could remember having done, I was in finer physical condition than at any time since I was a schoolboy.

My mental reaction to these receptions, as I stood on the outside looking in on an industry where I once had been a figure, pleased me tremendously. I could look rejection and failure in the face, and if I didn't laugh them away at least I was able to muster a smile. I marveled at my complete disregard for drugs; not once did the old urge attack me. Only now, in these hours which once would have been intolerable, did I fully appreciate the wonders which Dr. Edgren and the Institute had worked in me.

Instead of falling apart at the seams, I kept trying. And in the meantime I found content in my blessings: Harriet's happiness, our children, our home, and my new found health. These, I knew, I would not trade for all the fame in the world nor would I jeopardize them again in the mire of discontent and frustration.

It had taken me too many years to obtain the peace and contentment which springs from within and now I was also able to seek refuge in prayer. This is not to say that I had become overly religious, but God had not failed me in my most desperate hour and I knew I could never fail Him again.

I also discovered, with relieved and almost unbelievable amazement, that I had learned to live with pain. One day, when I had walked too much in visiting the studios and came away with raw patches on my stump as well as the usual frustrating rejections, my leg began to pain with a violence which previously would have driven me to a doctor for a morphine injection. The thought never occurred to me, this time or on later similar occasions. I simply clenched my teeth, drove home, made myself as comfortable as possible on the living room couch, and forgot my misery over a cup of tea with Harriet.

It still was necessary for me to have continual kidney checkups against the possibility of a kidney tumor recurrence. But the first time I went for one of those painful cystoscopys, I made certain that henceforth and forevermore there would be no pain-killing injections.

"I'll leave word that you are to have no injections of any kind nor any sleeping pills," the doctor agreed.

"We'll be even more careful than that," I told him firmly. "Every time it is necessary for me to undergo a checkup I want it written emphatically on my chart that absolutely there are to be no injections or sleeping medicine under any conditions. That way some young intern with a kind heart won't make the mistake of trying to spare me some pain."

The doctor followed my orders and I realized with astonishment that the occasional cystoscopys were not so painful as I had imagined through all those years of torment. Actually they became less and less of an ordeal until they were no more annoying to me than fretting in a barber chair is to some men.

How strange the workings of the mind and its effect on the body. For gradually, the kidney attacks became fewer and farther between, and where once I was passing two or more stones each year, two years passed without a single stone.

Another factor which proved conclusively to me the extent of my rehabilitation was my ability to discuss freely the ordeal I had been through. This was brought home to me with astounding force when Hy Gardner, columnist for the New York *Herald Tribune,* invited me to be a guest on his television program. On the show I was able to speak freely of my troubles; I had been ill and that was that.

Meanwhile, almost two months passed. Money was no immediate problem; I had earned great sums and saved conscientiously. Yet it was a seeming eternity of inactivity which passed before finally I received a call in February from station WINS in New York.

They offered me a spot as a disc jockey from seven to ten in the morning, and while it wasn't exactly what I desired it was a start up the road back and I was tremendously grateful for the opportunity to take this first step in the right direction.

This show, which we called Contact, was patterned after Bill Cullen's highly-successful Pulse, an NBC program. While it was only a local show I worked on it as diligently as I had on any of my network programs of the past.

It was an unbelievable boost to my morale when *Variety*

gave us a pat on the back. This review, which did so much for me, said:

March 6, 1957

When the ailing Bill Stern left the air several months ago he left as a veteran sportscaster. He returned last week via WINS as a deejay, interviewer and general radio raconteur. It was a humorless Stern who held the many facets of "Contact" together, but he nonetheless brought a vibrancy into a nicely disciplined three hours on the second day of the new show. . . .

In better than the hour heard, Stern, who is an excellent interviewer, exchanged thoughts by beep phone with Marie Torre, *Herald Trib* TV columnist, Paramount theater entrepreneur Bob Shapiro and others. A number of columnists from the local papers, like Miss Torre, will be regulars on the stanza. There's Phillip Strassburg, nightclub beater from the *Mirror,* and Leo Shull from *Show Business,* covering the local boite-legit-motion pic scene. It was a clever idea nicely consummated when Miss Torre, with Stern occasionally interjecting questions, gave a rundown of the big shows the night before on TV.

Her commentary was lucid and honest. The honesty extended to another show regular, Maggi McNellis, who has been with WINS since last fall. Miss McNellis, taking most of the 9:30-9:45 seg of the program, expanded cleverly on the Benny Goodman opening at the Waldorf. It wasn't all peaches and cream, this sing-song word stylist praised much, lambasted a little and added a clear picture of the celebrities present and the Empire Room decor and management. In most of what generally was heard on the show there were items worthy of the trade's sometime attention. Five minutes of news on the half-hour was well done, especially by Stan Burns, show's chief "Mr. Outside."

Lacking sponsors of his own, maestro Stern gave frequent pitches of a minute or more in length for WINS' 10 A.M.

"Kash Box," money giveaway. Miss McNellis lent herself to a similar pitch. It's distressing to hear a stanza, with considerable potential, demean itself by inordinately long hypoes for a show far below it on the radio ladder of prestige.

Throughout the summer I did this show for WINS, and while I was treated with extreme kindness I realized that I was only on the fringe of a business which still was and always will be my life's blood. Local operations were a new facet to me in view of the fact that where I had spent dollars before, now only pennies were available. This was no fault of WINS, it being the nature of the business for a local station.

Then, on a memorable day in August I received a telephone call from Mike Roshkind, who was handling public relations for Mutual Broadcasting System.

"Bill," he asked, "how would you like to do a sports show for Mutual?"

I could hardly answer at first because of my excitement. The words seemed to jam in my throat, tumbling over each other in their eagerness to get out. Mike's words were among the most beautiful I had ever heard because they meant my re-entry into the network field and into sports, the branch of the industry I had always preferred.

Details were worked out swiftly and in September, 1957, I was back on the network with Mutual doing a nightly show. In the past I would have been surrounded by assistants. This time, so happy was I to return, I did it all myself —writing, producing, and broadcasting.

The following January will always be one of the most memorable months of my life. My old sponsor, Colgate, for whom I had worked twelve years putting on the fantastically successful Sports Newsreel, proved its intense loyalty to me once again when it brought me, coast to coast, twice each morning over the Mutual network. It was a heartening vote of confidence which I shall never forget.

Then, although I had only been back on the air in sports for three short months, the nation's radio editors voted me the *Radio and TV Daily* award as the sportscaster of the year.

Hy Gardner, on whose show I had appeared in those days of unemployed trepidation following my discharge from Hartford, greeted this announcement with a story in the New York *Herald Tribune*. He wrote:

> January 21, 1958
>
> I'll bet Bill Stern got the kick of his life Monday morning when he was awakened by a telegram from *Radio and TV Daily* informing him that some 600 editors voted Stern "Radio's Sportscaster of the Year."
>
> Less than a year ago Bill agreed to appear on our television interview show and courageously recalled the months he spent trying to regain his mental health in a Hartford rest home. The story he told sent chills up the spine and made you wonder how anyone can resume what we call normal living after a round trip to and from the dark dungeon of mental collapse. Bill, with an iron will, returned to broadcasting several months after his psychiatrists gave him the green light.
>
> It gives a friend a warm feeling on a frigid afternoon to be able to report Stern's victory.
>
> In addition to "Sportscaster of the Year" I'd add another encomium—I'd like to call Bill Stern's return to action the Comeback of the Year.

I savored Gardner's words, which seemed somehow to keynote what was a completely new form of life for me. My early Colgate shows necessitated my rising at four o'clock in the morning, Monday through Friday. Then came quiet, serene early morning drives to the studio so that I was there in time for a 5:30 A.M. rehearsal and by 6:25 A.M. I could be on the air.

This meant that I arrived home before midday and Harriet and I had the entire afternoon together. It was a quiet life we chose. Once again I discovered the joys of reading as Harriet, long an avid reader, introduced me to the "good books."

But I found that my tastes ran to the action in Civil War history and the biographies of people in the entertainment world. On weekends, when I did not have to go to the studio, we began regularly to enjoy Broadway shows together.

We were content in a manner I had never known, and I found, too, that I didn't have to press aggressively to be a success. Another firm step forward came when I was selected by WPIX, the television station of the New York *Daily News*, to do the pregame road shows which preceded the New York Yankee baseball telecasts during the 1958 season.

Apparently I had made it back. And yet there still were more hurdles to clear.

In the fall of 1958 Mutual decided to do an All-Service schedule of football games played by the Army, Navy, and Air Force academies. The series was sponsored by Philco and I was assigned to the games.

I was stunned and incredulous when Mutual received letters from both Captain Slade Cutter and Colonel Earl Blaik, athletic directors respectively at the naval and military academies, that they did not want me to handle the games.

Irate thoughts that the old prejudices were at work leaped into my mind. But these were replaced immediately by the face of Dr. Edgren and again I could hear him saying: "The best thing to do is to ignore it. Don't let it get under your skin. Hold your tongue, turn your other cheek, and pray."

Then, too, I realized on calmer consideration I wasn't certain that this was a result of prejudice. Let's not start imagining things I warned myself. So, quite calmly, I went to Blair Walliser, executive vice-president of Mutual, and offered to give up the assignment.

"Just sit tight," Walliser advised me.

Then he telephoned both of the academies and told them that I was the choice of both Mutual and Philco and asked them why they were objecting to my doing the games. After talking to them, Walliser called me back into his office.

"Bill," he said, "they told me that there was nothing personal in their objections but that they had received so many complaints about your work in the past few years that they simply didn't feel you were up to the assignment."

What could I say of those past years? I merely nodded.

"Anyhow," he added, "they have agreed to stand by and judge you on the basis of your work at present."

How glad I was that I had held my tongue. Once again I offered a silent prayer of thanks for Dr. Edgren. Given the opportunity I knew that I could make good. Happily, I can say that I did. In a few weeks, Walliser called me in again.

"Both Army and Navy have advised me," he smiled, "that you sound as good as you did fifteen years ago. They have withdrawn all objections, and on top of that they want you to handle the Army-Navy game."

It was redemption, and yet it wasn't entirely complete until that cold December day in Philadelphia when, as I sat in the broadcasting booth between halves of the Army-Navy game, Cutter came in and stuck out his hand.

"I'm glad you're well, Bill," he said. "I was only doing my job and now it's a pleasure to be able to tell you that you are doing a great one on yours."

Shaking hands with him I no longer felt the numbing iciness of the afternoon. Suddenly I was warm all over from the glow coursing through my veins.

There have been a number of comforting, strengthening moments such as these in the blessed days since then.

New encouragement was provided when *TV Radio Mirror* magazine informed me early in 1959 that I had won its award as the previous year's favorite radio sports announcer. This I prize highly because it is the only award based on a nationwide poll of listeners. The magazine blurb under my picture made me feel, almost, as if I had never been away.

> What more can we say about Bill Stern, [it said.] He's captured your votes since 1947 when he won our very first poll . . . Is still in there pitching the "inside stuff."

To cap it all there was a letter from Dr. Francis J. Braceland, psychiatrist-in-chief at The Institute of Living in Hartford. It made me tremendously proud, and grateful.

> Dear Bill:
>
> The excellent reports that I get about you from Dr. Edgren and the things that I read about your accomplishments give me a great feeling of satisfaction. You have done an excellent job. You are to be sincerely congratulated and I am so delighted to see you back in the swing of things.
>
> Although it is impossible to convey to each person who is here our feelings and hopes, nonetheless we are vitally interested in their welfare. Without this interest, the job here would be impossible.
>
> Please know, therefore, that by your accomplishments you help a great many people. You encourage those who are having trouble themselves and who have learned that you had difficulty and saw it through, and you also encourage the members of the staffs like ours who feel that the efforts that this work requires are not in vain.
>
> With my own sincere personal congratulations and the

congratulations and prayers and best wishes of every member of the staff, I am

Sincerely,

Francis J. Braceland, M.D.

I cherish that letter and a deep gratitude wells up within me at the kindness of people; the ever-aiding votes of the most distant and anonymous listener, the encouragement of the awards, the inspiration of such earnest men as Dr. Braceland and the remarkable Dr. Edgren, a great man to whom I owe a debt I shall never be able to repay, as well as the helpful efforts of all those who have smoothed that pitted path back from nowhere.

Above all I cherish my loved ones for their faith, help, and understanding.

How can I ever repay Harriet for standing beside me so gallantly through those long years of torture and misery and for cleansing me of the taste of ashes which I knew at that moment when life was at its lowest ebb and my last bridge seemingly had been burned behind me?

How does a man apologize and explain his too human weaknesses and frailties to the children he adores, so that they can understand and be unashamed?

All I can say to them, now that it is over, is thank you.

And thank God.

Epilogue

Better is the end of a thing than the beginning thereof.

—Ecclesiastes 7.8

BILL STERN'S LOVELY HOME in Purchase, New York, is a house of contentment; a friendly fortress secure in the knowledge that it has weathered a greater storm than fate possibly could conjure again.

Here you meet a well-knit family. Bill and Harriet Stern cherish their children: black-haired, energetic Peter; pretty Mary May with her love of horses; and pert, red-haired, apple-cheeked Patty.

Harriet, slim, vivacious, and more serenely beautiful than ever in their great victory, carefully tends the flowers in her tiny, enchanted greenhouse; curls up contentedly with a book on the cheerful side porch; serves tea before the welcoming fireplace in the wide-windowed living room; or presides merrily as Bill and Peter play billiards in the friendly family room.

When the weather is warm Bill lies, utterly relaxed, in a hammock beside the bright blue swimming pool, the scarred stump which is a monument to the grimmest days of his life basking unashamedly in the sunlight. Four frisky miniature French poodles whine and bark until he cradles them in his arms or yap noisily along the side of the pool as he swims lazily through the cool waters.

The velvet voice, like wine, has mellowed and become richer with the passage of time. The relentless aggression has been obliterated by a gentle humility and the brown eyes sparkle, their one-time glitter gone. The ready rapier in the patent leather scabbard is no more. A new strength and sureness prophesy that his rich talents will be ever more in demand.

Bill Stern has made it home.